# What people are saying about Confidence: How to build the confidence you need to enjoy your life:

"This book tackles something dear to our hearts; the call to live our lives to the full, with confidence. The pages are packed with practical wisdom and the words are presented in an accessible style that makes it a joy to read and a gift to treasure"

—Veronica Ellis, Artist and Owner, Nature's Grace

"Confidence can be a slippery varmint. It can come and go in different areas of life and through all times in life. What Cathy Sirett does in her book, Complete Confidence, is bring a calm clarity to the topic. Her ideas are deep in understanding but also easy to relate to. As a writer myself, I appreciate the skill it takes to describe complicated ideas in simple ways. Her examples are engaging, and the manner of writing is light and positive, while carrying a very important message, with techniques easy to apply to life. The book is like a wander through a garden, a progressive, logical path to a place you want to be, written in an easy conversational tone. Recommended without reservation, this book is an affirmational method of uncovering the best within us."

—Anna Blake, Horse Advocate and Author

# COMPLETE CONFIDENCE:

## HOW TO BUILD THE CONFIDENCE YOU NEED TO ENJOY YOUR LIFE

### CATHY SIRETT

AUTHOR ACADEMY elite

Copyright © 2018 Cathy Sirett
All rights reserved

Printed in the United States of America and the United Kingdom

Published by Author Academy Elite,
P.O. Box 43, Powell, OH 43035

www.AuthorAcademyElite.com

All rights reserved. No part of this publication may be reproduced, stored in a retrieval system or transmitted in any form or by any means—for example, electronic, photocopy, recording—without the prior written permission of the publisher. The only exception is brief quotations in printed reviews.

Paperback ISBN: 978-1-64085-430-7

Hardback ISBN: 978-1-64085-431-4

E-book ISBN: 978-1-64085-432-1

Library of Congress Control Number: 2018956781

*'Optimism is the faith that leads to achievement. Nothing can be done without hope and confidence'*
Helen Keller, Author, Activist and Academic

**Confidence:**
From the Latin *con-fidere*: with trust

**Unconfidence:**
Un`con´fi`dence
Noun: Absence of confidence; uncertainty; doubt.
*Webster's Revised Unabridged Dictionary*

**Unconfident:**
Adjective: Not confident; hesitant.
*Oxford Dictionaries.com*

# TABLE OF CONTENTS

Foreword — xi
Acknowledgements — xiii
Introduction — xv

## PART 1
### YOUR CONFIDENCE JOURNEY: THE FIVE PROVEN AND PRACTICAL STEPS TO BUILDING CONFIDENCE

| | | |
|---|---|---|
| Chapter 1 | Step 1: Why is your Confidence Journey important? | 3 |
| Chapter 2 | Step 2: Where are you starting from? | 9 |
| Chapter 3 | Step 3: What is your destination, and what are your options for getting there? | 19 |
| Chapter 4 | Step 4: What about obstacles and challenges? | 33 |
| Chapter 5 | Step 5: How to make sure you get there | 43 |

# PART 2
## EXPANDING YOUR CONFIDENCE ZONE

| | | |
|---|---|---|
| Chapter 6 | How to stop getting in your own way | 55 |
| Chapter 7 | How to switch on confidence in those moments when you need it | 67 |
| Chapter 8 | How to negotiate with Confidence Kidnappers | 75 |
| Chapter 9 | How to use your fear to expand your Confidence Zone | 85 |
| Chapter 10 | Weird and wonderful ways other people have expanded their Confidence Zones | 99 |

# PART 3
## CONFIDENCE TRAPS AND TIPS:
## FIVE TRAPS TO AVOID AND FIVE TIPS TO ACCELERATE YOUR CONFIDENCE JOURNEY

### Confidence Traps to avoid

| | | |
|---|---|---|
| Trap 1 | Pushing through: Why 'just doing it' doesn't always work — and when it sometimes does! | 109 |
| Trap 2 | Missing the bigger picture: The rest of your life matters too | 111 |
| Trap 3 | Kisses and kittens: The friends that keep you frightened | 114 |
| Trap 4 | Heroes and gurus: How The Guru Syndrome stops you getting true confidence | 118 |
| Trap 5 | Faux amis: False friends, when confidence may not be what it seems | 123 |

**Confidence Journey accelerator tips**

| | | |
|---|---|---|
| Tip 1 | Know yourself: What's your blind spot? | 129 |
| Tip 2 | Know yourself: Who's in control? | 134 |
| Tip 3 | Know yourself: How to be mindful — and why it matters to our confidence | 140 |
| Tip 4 | Be grateful: The attitude of gratitude | 146 |
| Tip 5 | Practice makes perfect: At least *deliberate* practice does | 150 |

# PART 4
## HOW TO HELP SOMEONE ELSE ON THEIR CONFIDENCE JOURNEY: THE SEVEN GOLDEN RULES

| | | |
|---|---|---|
| Rule 1 | Be a role model | 156 |
| Rule 2 | Ask permission | 158 |
| Rule 3 | Be truly 'other-focused' | 160 |
| Rule 4 | Commit to your own development | 162 |
| Rule 5 | Be honest | 163 |
| Rule 6 | Make it a two-way street | 166 |
| Rule 7 | Know when to get help yourself | 167 |

# PART 5
## SUSTAINING CONFIDENCE: THREE KEYS TO STAYING CONFIDENT — AND ENJOYING YOUR LIFE

| | | |
|---|---|---|
| Key 1 | The Confidence Wheel | 171 |
| Key 2 | Balance | 177 |
| Key 3 | Giving yourself permission. This is the 'Just one more thing' for the whole book! | 180 |

About the Author     189

# FOREWORD

If I told you that developing your own confidence was possible, to really be able to tackle something that makes you full of anxiety, and to do it with a sense of calm and grace—and do it on your own, would you believe me? I wouldn't have believed it was possible myself; in fact I was skeptical even while working with Cathy Sirett in person! Through our time together, however, I was able to see glimpses of that path forward; the path towards developing my own confidence. Cathy brought years of experience in the professional world, stories of new and innovative approaches to problem-solving, and used those techniques and principles to help me unlock my confident self from within. By telling myself "I should be able to…" and "just push through it, it'll get better with practice…" I had not addressed the core of what was creating my anxiety, now was I listening to my own inner-voice on what could legitimately make it better. In our sessions together I saw, with Cathy's guidance, that in honoring the fear and finding a small experiment, that I could expand my capabilities and the zone in which I truly felt confident. What was remarkable, was how with this combination of storytelling, techniques, and pragmatic practice, I was able to tackle other areas where I was lacking confidence. I translated my in-person work with Cathy around confidence in progressing my classical dressage practice, into increased confidence at work and in inter-personal relationships. The challenges may have seemed insurmountable, and the solutions and techniques Cathy taught me may have seemed overly simple—yet the small shifts helped me uncover the key to unlocking my fully confident self.

In this book, Cathy lays out the invaluable methods and exercises that will help you on your journey to confidence. Whether you are just embarking on the journey to find your most confident self, or are looking for an additional tool-set to further improve yourself—this book will deliver what you need for sustained, self-directed progress to a confident you. With the book, and the wealth of materials available at the companion website, you will be able to realize your confidence goal—be it around public speaking, navigating change at work, having difficult conversations about family budgets—wherever you feel 'un-confident', these resources will help.

Providing the tools to really do this yourself is a novel idea, and one that promises to have an impact on any of us that find moments where we wish we were more confident. Simple concepts, small shifts, expert tools and guidance, all combining to create a self-directed and successful path to finding your truly confident and effective self.

Christie A. Fisher, MBA;
Director of Business Planning, Microsoft

# ACKNOWLEDGEMENTS

There is a common image of a writer being the lone artist working by themselves in a tiny attic room, isolated from the world, friends and family. However, anyone who has ever actually produced a book knows that it is not a one person job. Being an author takes a team, and I have had the best team behind me all the way on this project. There are so many people who have influenced me in my own journey to producing this book I cannot possibly hope to name them all, but there are a few key team members I want to mention.

First, I need to thank the College Farm Crew (Ruth Drake Chapman, Sue Tolliday and Janet Sayles) who have provided practical and emotional support. You gave me the time to focus on the writing when many other things needed doing, and listened patiently (at least on the outside!) to every new idea as it happened.

Second, I have had many volunteer proofreaders who have made this book as good as it is including Kas Fitzpatrick, Ange Riley, Sarah Le Vallois, and Isabelle Zeimet. You not only identified punctuation errors and typos, but spotted some of my less appealing writing habits which I was able to fix before the book came out in print—thank you. Particular thanks go to Veronica Ellis for her amazing job as editor, offering not just basic advice but insights which have made the book so much stronger.

Thirdly, to my "tribe" on facebook, the Complete Confidence Launch Team, whose enthusiasm for what I was doing, and responses to my vlogs kept me going during the tougher times. Knowing you were there, listening, engaging and responding made the experience so much less about "me writing a book" and more about "I am doing this to bring value to people", which is immensely more motivating.

I also want to acknowledge the importance of my family: David Sirett, Liz Spencer and Kev Spencer who made sure I had some down time and came back refreshed for the major chore of editing as well as being cheerleaders and supporters in the years leading to this project.

The wonderful graphics in this book are the work of designer John Gaudin, and the cover work credit goes to Debbie Byrne of Jetlaunch.

There are three more groups to thank:

- the Igniting Souls Tribe of Author Academy Elite who are possibly the most powerful support group I have ever come across,
- The team of Complete Confidence Coaches who have invested their time and effort to be ready to work with you on your Confidence Journeys (Debbie Reilly, Suz Crichton-Stuart, Lesley Jennings and Merry Clark)

And lastly, everyone who has ever worked with me on confidence concerns. It is thanks to your courage in facing up to your anxieties and fears and asking for help that this book exists at all.

Yours, in confidence

Cathy Sirett

# INTRODUCTION

Hello and welcome to my book! **Complete Confidence: How to build the confidence you need to enjoy your life.**

That title sounds ambitious. That's because this book *is* ambitious. It is also based on reality: in my 25 years as a coach and consultant I have helped many people go from being anxious and fearful to enjoying their lives with confidence. From corporate executives to consultants, from artists to accountants, from horse-riders to people just wanting to enjoy their hobbies without anxiety—I have coached them all to a level of authentic confidence and happiness they weren't sure was possible. That's what this book will do for you.

## Why did I write this book?

The simple answer is, "Because I have been there!". I know what it's like to feel physically sick at the thought of making a presentation at work, to not even apply for a place on a really exciting project team because I did not have the confidence, to not go to a friend's party for fear of having to meet and talk to strangers. I have also stood in a courtyard holding the lead rope to one of the slowest, safest horses in the stables crying my eyes out because I was too frightened to ride. I looked for help. I did all the things I was told to do to build my confidence: I went to workshops, I did courses and I became an expert in positive visualisation. Some of them worked, for a short time. Sooner or later though, the anxiety and fear would return and I would be back where I started but, this time, also feeling a failure because I couldn't 'fix it'.

Over time, I did become confident making presentations, signing up for project teams and in life in general. I also became confident enough as a rider to become a Confidence Coach for other equestrians. It's been a long Confidence Journey for me, but over the years I have refined it to a straightforward process that works. What I have done and helped others do is in this book. It wasn't always easy, but the basic process *is* simple. Simple to understand, but not always easy to do. How many things in life are like that? It may take some effort, it may take some time. The one thing I will say is: it will work.

People ask me, "Are you 100% confident all the time now?". I laugh and say, "No, but I know what to do when I feel unconfident, and I know how to build authentic confidence in any situation and that's great!".

This book shares with you what I have learned along the way. It is based on how hundreds of people have created their own Confidence Journeys to rediscover enjoyment in their work and in their lives. In here you will find tools, insights and lots of examples of exactly *how* people have built their confidence.

Are you ready to start work on creating your *own* Confidence Journey now?

## How to use this book:

You can use it any way you like really, after all, it's your life and your Confidence Journey. Let me share what's in it and then you can decide how you want to use it.

The book has five sections:

## Part 1
## Your Confidence Journey: The five proven and practical steps to building confidence.

Start here if you have a confidence issue or situation you want to deal with right now. This section gives you the simple framework for building your Confidence Journey and will make a real difference to you right away. This is the core of the book: if all you take away from reading this book is how to use these 5 steps to build your own Confidence Journey then you win!

## Part 2
## Expanding your Confidence Zone: Tried and tested ways to make your Confidence Zone bigger over time.

Read this section for the 'aha!' moments that will enable you to grow your Confidence Zone to cover more and more situations, more and more issues, and equip you to be your own best Confidence Coach.

There are lots of examples and stories here so you can see how real people have made real differences in their lives with their understanding and work.

## Part 3
## Confidence Traps and Tips: Five traps to avoid and five tips to accelerate your Confidence Journey

This is a section most people read when they have some time with a cup of tea or coffee and want to know more about what makes their Confidence Journey easier—or harder.

Here you will learn the five biggest Confidence Traps, and what to do about them. There are also five Confidence Tips with stories of how people have accelerated their Confidence Journey by understanding more about confidence and how it works.

## Part 4

## How to help someone else with their Confidence Journey: The seven golden rules

One thing that happens when we build our own confidence is that other people see this, and ask us for advice. Because confidence is such a personal thing, I share some of the best advice out there about how to support someone else on their Confidence Journey in a genuine way that will help make a real difference to them.

## Part 5

## Sustaining confidence: Three keys to staying confident — and enjoying your life

In this section I share how people sustain their confidence over time. I give you the Confidence Wheel, the concept of balance and the cardinal rule to 'Give yourself permission'. These will make sure we *stay* confident, and continue to enjoy our lives.

Are you ready?

Let's get started…

# PART 1
## YOUR CONFIDENCE JOURNEY: THE FIVE PROVEN AND PRACTICAL STEPS TO BUILDING CONFIDENCE

Your Confidence Journey is how you learn to make the transition from where you are now (unconfident) to where you want to be (confident) and it has five steps:

**STEP 1** Why is this Confidence Journey important?

**STEP 2** Where are we starting from?

*unsureness*
**Port of Unconfidence**
*uncertainty*

**STEP 3** What is your destination, and what are your options for getting there?

**STEP 4** What about obstacles and challenges?

**STEP 5** How to make sure you get there

*contentment*
**Port of Confidence**
*enjoyment*

# CHAPTER 1
## STEP 1: WHY IS YOUR CONFIDENCE JOURNEY IMPORTANT?

*"Nothing changes until you do."* Mike Robbins, Leadership Expert and Author

### Unconfidence is sneaky

It creeps up on us without our realising. It disguises itself as 'common sense' or 'being sensible'. It hides under the label of 'Don't set yourself up for failure', or 'Protect yourself from disappointment'. Unconfidence is often invisible—until it changes your life. And it does change your life. If you are reading this book it probably already has.

Sarah and Sioned were two top performing managers of local branches of a successful banking company. Both had come through the ranks and were now seen as role models for women in their organisation. Both had replied to an invitation to speak at the National Banking Conference about how they had achieved so much with identical phrases, "Love to, but I am afraid with end of year, we are just too busy to be able to prepare to the standard required.". Too busy? Too busy to prepare and deliver a presentation to the whole national organisation? At a conference where the key decision makers of the company would be in the audience?

When I talked privately to them, they still claimed that workload meant it would be impossible. However, with supportive coaching they also revealed that even if they had the time, they were not excited about the opportunity. In fact, they admitted, they were terrified. It is one thing to manage a team of people you know, and lead them in the day-to-day operations of a branch. It is quite another to think about standing on a stage in front of a thousand people.

At first, both of them said, "It doesn't really matter, there are plenty of people who want to present.". However, as we reflected on the successful career paths of previous speakers, and the challenges they were both facing in moving beyond being branch managers into more central and strategic roles, they began to see that *not* presenting would have a huge negative impact on their careers, and lives. Suddenly, for both of them, building a Confidence Journey that would enable them to do these presentations became critical. And they were ready to start.

## Unconfidence helps us

One thing to know about feeling unconfident, or even afraid, is that it is just our brain's way of trying to keep us safe. When you feel nervous, worried, or frightened about something, this is the way your unconscious mind has of saying, "Don't do this!" or, "You're not safe doing this!". If you think about it, this is a very useful mechanism to have. When you sprain an ankle, your brain quickly realises that relying on that foot is not sensible, and so kicks in with its 'safety management' plan and makes sure you don't put weight on it while it is healing. Even without thinking, you will find yourself doing most things with the other, healthy foot. This is your unconscious at work. Another example is when you are a child, and put a hand in the fire, you learn that it hurts. From then on you don't even really have to think about it, you don't put your hand in flames again.

Sometimes, however, this wonderful survival mechanism gets in the way. I remember when I sprained my ankle, and discovered over a *year* later, that I was still favouring my other leg and not putting my full weight on the 'injured' one. My brain had developed a habit of protecting my sprained leg, and I had never corrected it. This is why physiotherapy is so often needed after an injury, to teach the body that it can work properly again.

Think about some of your anxieties: often they stem from actual experiences. Simon applied for a project team he knew would help his career. His application was rejected and he was bitterly disappointed. The next time an opportunity came up, he told himself there was no point applying as he wouldn't get it anyway.

Our unconscious tries to keep us safe, but it doesn't differentiate between physical, emotional or mental harm. It will fight just as hard to protect us from embarrassment and disappointment as from actual physical injury. Simon's unconscious was keeping him safe from feeling that disappointment again.

This conversation was an "Aha!" moment for Emma. Emma had always been an enthusiastic horsewoman. She had never had a bad fall, and yet recently she had noticed she was not riding as much and seemed to be finding excuses not to ride. Sometimes she was 'too busy', or the weather was 'too windy', or it just didn't feel right today. When she realised it had been three months since she had ridden (and she used to ride every day!) she got in touch with me. We had a long conversation, exploring lots of possibilities. After about twenty minutes she suddenly stopped talking, and looked away, recalling an incident that had happened about four months earlier. There had been a big family party and at that event every family member had loudly and publicly criticised her passion, repeating the phrase, "What's the point in doing it if you aren't going to be the best? You're just setting yourself up for disappointment!".

At the time she had just smiled and laughed it off, but now she realised that the message had actually landed somewhere in her mind (probably because it was a common one often repeated in her family throughout her whole life). From that day her unconscious had decided to keep her safe from that disappointment and the best way to do that was to stop her from riding. Once we uncovered this, we were able to identify *why* starting her Confidence Journey mattered to her and what the focus of it should be.

Our unconscious mind acts very instinctively and often without any connection with our conscious mind. Bringing the behaviour of our unconscious mind into our conscious mind is a key step in realising *why* unconfidence matters to us and *why* we need to address it. Because unconfidence is about keeping us safe, we don't want to ignore it, or shut it down. We want to make sure that whatever we do to become confident also keeps us safe, so we need to get our conscious and unconscious minds working together. The Latin roots of the word confidence mean 'with trust', so we want to get our conscious and unconscious minds trusting each other, then we can trust ourselves. This is exactly what we will do on this Confidence Journey.

Take a moment to ask yourself: How is *your* unconfidence impacting your life right now and what are you *not* doing because you lack confidence? Hold those thoughts, as this will be the issue you can take on your Confidence Journey.

## Unconfidence can be measured

Once we are aware of our unconfidence in an area, and we know we want to do something about it, the next question is: how will we know when we are making progress? When we go on any other type of journey, we know how far it will be so we can see the progress we are making as time goes by. How can we do this with confidence?

Simple: we can use a scale of 0-10. 0 in this case is *zero unconfidence*. So it's an unconfidence scale, not a confidence one. Why do it this way round? For me, confidence is our natural state: when we are born we are all innately confident. It is only over time that our natural confidence can erode and unconfidence creeps in. It's only right that we reflect this natural state of confidence by having our zero state, or neutral state be 'totally confident'. If 0 is totally confident then it fits that 10 is totally unconfident. All our fears and anxieties lie somewhere along that scale. Once we have decided *why* we are unconfident, and why it matters to us, then we give a number to this level of unconfidence and we can use that to measure our progress on our Confidence Journey.

Think about the issue you came up with earlier in this chapter: what unconfidence score would you give to that issue? Don't worry too much about being 100% right as long as you come up with a working number we can use it in Step 2: Where are you starting from?

## Just one more thing

## Self awareness is a prerequisite for self management

This is one of my favourite sayings. We can't expect to manage ourselves if we aren't aware of what is impacting us. Step 1 of your Confidence Journey is all about being aware of the impact your lack of confidence is having on your life. It might be impacting your work, your home life or your enjoyment of life. Whatever it is impacting, being aware that a lack of confidence is responsible is the first step to managing it.

Here are some questions for you before taking the next step:

- How is your confidence issue impacting your life right now?
- What are you *not* doing because of your lack of confidence?
- What is your unconfidence score on this issue?

# CHAPTER 2
## STEP 2: WHERE ARE YOU STARTING FROM?

*"Start where you are. Use what you have. Do what you can."*
— Arthur Ashe, Tennis Champion

*"It's impossible to map out a route to your destination unless you know where you are starting from."* — Suze Orman, Author and Motivational Speaker

In any journey we make, it's great to have a map. Whether that's on a SatNav, a smartphone or on an ocean chart, having a map that shows where we are starting from, and where we want to end up is essential. If it also shows different options for getting from one place to another that makes it even more useful. Guess what? We can do that for our confidence too.

One of the first things I struggled with whenever I worked on my own confidence, was in trying to define exactly what it was I was unconfident about. I knew I was worried about a presentation, or a project—but I didn't know how to be more specific than that. This meant that when my friends and family offered me solutions, they didn't quite 'fit' and I struggled to find any route out of my unconfidence. Then I realised that building confidence is a journey, and with any journey, we start by knowing where we are on the map. That's what this chapter is about: how can we identify where we are starting from and be specific enough to set ourselves up for success in reaching our destination? Sometimes, you realise that where you are actually starting from is somewhere very different from where you thought you were starting from...

This is **Confidence Mapping**.

There are 3 actions in creating your Confidence Map:

## Action 1: Create your worksheet

On the Complete Confidence website there are templates of all the worksheets we develop and use in this book. However, for now I want you to create your own. When we actually create our own worksheet, it engages different parts of the brain than if we use a pre-printed one. That will make a difference in how your brain retains and uses the information on your map. Even today, when I am working with my coaching clients on confidence issues, I still have them draw their own Confidence Maps as it has such a different impact to using a prepared template.

Take a blank sheet of paper, I often just take a page out of the printer paper tray, and put a dot in the centre of it.

- Write a 0 next to that dot. That is our 'zero point', our natural, confident state.
- Draw two straight lines going through that point: one vertical and one horizontal.
- Starting at the 0, go halfway along to the right on the horizontal line and put a dot there with the number 5 next to it.
- Do the same to the left on the horizontal line.
- Place a dot with a 5 on the vertical line the same distance from the 0, both above and below the centre.

Now you can join those dots with a circle that goes through all four dots.

Next, at the ends of the horizontal line, put dots with 10 next to them and, again, place dots in the appropriate position on the vertical line, above and below the zero so you can create another circle linking the 10s.

The last stage is to now put dots on the lines where you think the number 8 would be and link these with another circle so you end up with this:

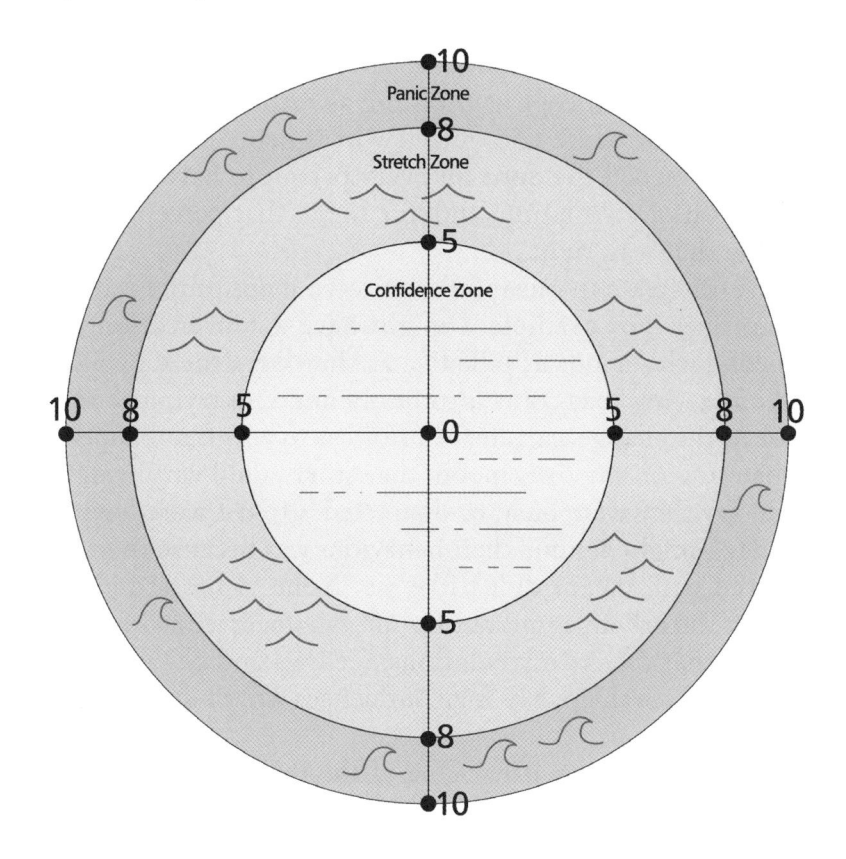

This is your **Confidence Map.**

What we have done is taken our linear scoring of our unconfidence and turned it into a visual where we can record everything about our issue and see how it looks as a whole.

This will make a real difference as you will see when we do actions 2 and 3.

## Action 2: Fill out your Confidence Map

Now we need to create your Confidence Map. In 1931 the Polish American Scientist and Philosopher, Alfred Korzybski, wrote a paper where he said, "The map is not the territory.". What he was saying was that whilst the territory, or world, might be real, our internal maps of the world are individual and created from our individual experiences and environments. It was a novel concept at the time as rather than the world being black or white and our view of it being either right or wrong, it opened the door for every person to have their own perception of a situation, and, for them, that perception was the one that was 'right'.

We all create in our minds, our own maps of the territory of our lives. For example, I might have a conversation with someone who is not as talkative as they were the day before, and on leaving that conversation my mind, in trying to make sense of the change, can create a story as to why that happened. Depending on my own mood, that story could vary widely. I could say they were busy, or distracted. Or, if I were having a bad day I might assume their behaviour was because they were annoyed with me, or didn't like me. None of those might be true for the other person but for me, whatever story I create is the one that affects my emotions, feelings and behaviour the next time I see them. My 'map' influences what I do, regardless of *their* map.

Why does this matter? One of the things I learned early on in my own confidence struggles was that everyone out there thinks they have the map that will solve my confidence issue!

Think about this: How many of us fear making presentations? (Hint: on most surveys it comes out as the second most stressful life event after bereavement). How many of us worry about taking on projects we are unsure of? How many of us have been scared or overwhelmed by events in our lives at some stage? And how many times has someone else, who also had those fears and worries assumed that *their* solution to their confidence issue would 'fix' us too?

It happens all the time and can actually make things worse. If a friend says what worked for them, and we try different things and none of them work for us then we can add a sense of being a failure to our list of anxieties. So it is important that we create our *own* map of our issue, and don't rely on someone else's map for our solutions. How do we do this?

Here's an example of a Confidence Map that one of my clients has allowed me to share here. On the website there are some other maps for a range of issues that you can look at too.

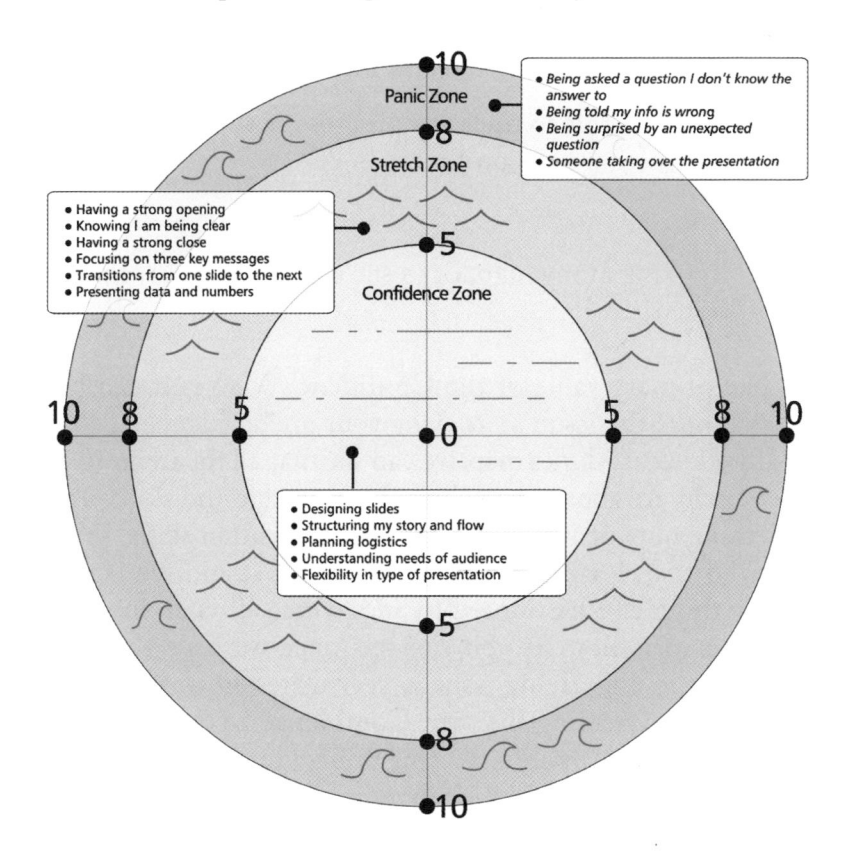

**Panic Zone (10)**
- Being asked a question I don't know the answer to
- Being told my info is wrong
- Being surprised by an unexpected question
- Someone taking over the presentation

**Stretch Zone (8)**
- Having a strong opening
- Knowing I am being clear
- Having a strong close
- Focusing on three key messages
- Transitions from one slide to the next
- Presenting data and numbers

**Confidence Zone (5)**
- Designing slides
- Structuring my story and flow
- Planning logistics
- Understanding needs of audience
- Flexibility in type of presentation

To fill this out, Mark thought about as many aspects of his issue as he could, he scored each aspect and then wrote it in the appropriate section on the map. When we talked in our coaching session, he added more aspects, those are the ones in italics on the map above. So now Mark has a visual of all the aspects of his confidence issue and we can now start looking at where his Confidence Journey starts.

## Action 3: Analyse your Confidence Map

What's the value of creating this Confidence Map? When I ask that question at workshops, I get several answers. The top three are always:

1. It shows me where I am starting from: where I *am* confident as well as where I am not.
2. I can use this to track my progress as things move from one section into another.

And…

3. Looking at my map, I can see patterns I hadn't realised were there.

The primary value of the Confidence Map is it can help you diagnose the issue *underlying* your unconfidence.

If we look at Mark's map, we can see that all the items in the inner circle, are about his technical knowledge and skills—and everything outside it is about his communication skills. When I noticed that, I asked him to think about it and see if there was anything else he wanted to add, which is when he added the items in italics. As you can see, once we have the items in italics, the underlying issue is very different to the one he started with. Creating his own Confidence Map helped him diagnose the *real* issue affecting him. He had thought his issue was 'presentation skills' when in fact, he was unconfident about *any* situation where he didn't feel in total control of the conversation. How interesting! It was a good thing we did the map otherwise Mark could have invested a lot of time and effort in fixing something that wasn't the real (underlying) issue.

In another example, which is shared on the website, Amanda used her Confidence Map to identify that her real issue was her anxiety about what other people think of her, and not anything to do with her ability to do her job effectively. Again if we had not done the map, we might have missed that and put a lot of time and effort into the wrong thing.

## Another use for the Confidence Map

There is, however, one more use for the Confidence Map: it stops you from making things worse. What do I mean by that? If we look at the Confidence Map, we see three circles. The first, inner circle, from 0-5, is the CONFIDENCE ZONE. Everything we do in here we are confident about doing, although as we approach 4 and 5 we might have to think about things a bit more than at 1 or 2. The third, outer circle, from 8-10, is the PANIC ZONE. Just the thought of doing anything in this zone makes us break out in a cold sweat. The second circle is the riskiest one when working with confidence. This circle, from 5-8, is the STRETCH ZONE: to do things here, we are really stretching our confidence. This is the zone where we can see something might be possible and we are tempted to grit our teeth and do it. After all, how bad could that be?

Very bad, it turns out. Here's the rule: every time we do something over a 5 (ie outside our Confidence Zone) we make things worse.

Soriya wasn't confident chairing her project team meetings, but believed that by doing it again and again she would build her confidence through the experience. What actually happened was that as time went by her nerves got worse. At every meeting, she was at a 7 or 8, gritting her teeth and pushing herself to do it, and each time she did that her unconscious learned that she was ignoring it and got louder. It got to the stage where she was being physically sick before each meeting and that was when she realised what was happening.

Breaking your confidence thresholds can lead to your unconscious shouting instead of just suggesting, and that isn't pleasant or useful. Am I saying that we should never do anything that we score over a 5? Yes, I am! Does that mean we are forever stuck only able to do the things on our map that are under 5? No, it doesn't. Because what we do when something scores above a 5, outside our Confidence Zone, is analyse it and come up with ways to bring it down to below a 5.

When Lucy realised that teaching a course to her co-workers put her at an 8 on her Confidence Map, she sat down and asked herself, "What has to happen to bring this down to a 5?". Using her map, she identified that her main fear was about having to be an 'expert' in front of her peers and how that would impact their working relationships. We redesigned the course to a series of interactive discussion groups addressing key questions and issues where the co-workers contributed and Lucy positioned herself as facilitator. With this structure, Lucy felt at a 3, well within her Confidence Zone, and confidently led the course.

## Just one more thing

### Comfort Zone versus Confidence Zone

Some people have asked - is a Confidence Zone the same as your Comfort Zone? The answer is no, it is not. Your Confidence Zone actually includes your Comfort Zone because in your Comfort Zone you are definitely confident but it also includes more. Your Comfort Zone is basically that small circle between 0 and 2, where you don't have to think about anything before doing it. The Confidence Zone is this *plus* where you are a 3-5, so you DO have to think a bit about how you do these activities, but are confident that you *can* do them.

You may have seen some of the memes about how you don't learn anything in your Comfort Zone, and they are right: learning and growth does not happen in the Comfort Zone, but it does happen in the outer edges of the CONFIDENCE

ZONE. Remember that: to learn, you need to be inside your Confidence Zone while outside your Comfort Zone. There are some examples of this in stories shared on the website.

Sometimes working out how to get things below a 5 isn't easy, but don't worry, in the next step of your Confidence Journey we have a process for making sure you have lots of options for doing exactly this!

Before we go there it's time for you to do your own Confidence Map. When you have done it, see what you can diagnose about yourself or, better still, find a friend you trust as a coach and have a conversation with them about it. For an example of a conversation around a Confidence Map, go to the Complete Confidence webpage at cathysirett.com.

# CHAPTER 3
## STEP 3: WHAT IS YOUR DESTINATION, AND WHAT ARE YOUR OPTIONS FOR GETTING THERE?

*"Would you tell me, please, which way I ought to go from here?"* asked Alice.
*"That depends a good deal on where you want to get to,"* said the Cat.
*"I don't much care where—"* said Alice.
*"Then it doesn't matter which way you go,"* said the Cat.
*"—so long as I get SOMEWHERE,"* Alice added as an explanation.
*"Oh, you're sure to do that,"* said the Cat, *"if you only walk long enough."*

from Alice's Adventures in Wonderland
by Lewis Carroll

Often paraphrased as

*"If you don't know where you're going then any road will get you there."*

When people say to me that they have lost their confidence, we often have a chat about how confidence is not a thing, or an object you can find or lose. It is a feeling, a sensation, a message from your unconscious to your conscious about how safe you truly feel with what you are planning to do. Remember, this is about trusting yourself. That is the definition of confidence from its Latin origins.

In the first exercise, you learned to analyse your feelings and to be aware of how confident or unconfident you feel when you are doing different things, defining the impact unconfidence is having on you and your life. When you did your Confidence Map you created a picture of everything you do around this issue and identified exactly where you *are* confident and where you are *not* confident—yet. This gives you your starting point on your Confidence Journey.

Now we can take this to the stage of planning our routes that will take us to our destination of Complete Confidence!

First, let's take a look at the five common mistakes people make when they try to find solutions for issues, or come up with strategies for tackling challenges. From my twenty years of experience working with top-level business people I can assure you, these mistakes are made by most of us. After I share the mistakes with you, I also share a fifteen minute IDEAS Process that will ensure we don't make any of them in our Confidence Journeys.

Here are the five biggest mistakes people make when they are developing strategies to deal with an issue they are not confident about.

## Mistake 1: Not identifying the issue in a useful way

I was working with a businessman, Daniel, who said he had been trying for years to fix one particular problem. I asked him what it was. He replied that his biggest problem was getting people to follow the correct procedures. The company made high specification parts used in medical equipment. Every night the machinery they used had to be carefully recalibrated to ensure they stayed within the required specifications. However, time after time the calibration team was coming in to find the machinery had not been turned off on time which meant it was too warm to do the calibration. This was costing the company a lot of money as more and more product was failing the quality testing. Daniel had tried running courses and training explaining it to his employees, he had one-to-one meetings with each line manager and they had then passed the message on to their teams, he had fined people who didn't follow procedure. He had even started disciplinary proceedings against some individuals leading to two employees being one step away from dismissal. None of this had fixed the problem. Daniel had clearly identified the problem as 'people are not following procedures', and spent a lot of time and effort trying to fix that.

I had a different perspective. I looked at the issue: the *real* issue was that the machines were not switched off at the right time. If we did that then the problem would not exist. I reframed the problem from, "How can we get people to remember about calibration?" to, "How can we make sure the machines are off at 7pm?". With that one single reframing of the problem, the answer was obvious: put the machines on a timer switch so they turned off automatically at 7pm. Problem solved.

You would think the manager would be happy with this cheap and quick fix, wouldn't you? Funnily enough, it took him a long time to accept this answer as he insisted that, "If only people would follow procedures we wouldn't need to buy these timers!". He was fixated on *his* definition of the issue rather than finding a useful way to look at the situation. Being able to 'reframe' things helps us find a useful way to look at things and makes it more possible to develop practical, effective strategies.

One thing you may notice about this reframing is that it turned the problem from something that *other* people had to change to asking what *we* could do to change. In other words, the only really useful way to look at a problem is to present it in a way where *we* have some ownership of it, where *we* have some control over the issue. Let me share an example: I could say, "My horse needs to stop barging me around, and start behaving properly.". Notice this puts all the responsibility on the horse to make a change. If I reframe this to, "I need to have some strategies for teaching my horse how I want him to behave around me." this is much more doable than the first way of framing the issue.

Similarly, I could say the issue is, "No one invites me onto their project teams anymore.", or I could reframe this as, " I don't know what to do to get invitations to the project teams I want to be on.".

So you can see that the first mistake people make is to not frame the issue in a useful, self-focused way.

## Mistake 2: Focus on the problem instead of the desired outcome

When we constantly focus on a problem, it grows. We notice every slight thing that makes it worse. Let's take someone saying, "I am scared about making a presentation." As an example, Anna had this problem, and sure enough, every time she tried do a presentation she was scared and proved it to herself all over again. Now, if we focused on her desired outcome, let's see how that might change things. A desired outcome is what it would look like if the problem were sorted out. In this case, the desired outcome turned out to be, "I will be able to make this specific presentation next month while remaining in my Confidence Zone.". Can you see how with this focus, instead of reminding ourselves how scared we are every time we think about making that presentation, we're already starting to think of things we *can* do to stay in our Confidence Zone?

This is particularly important when other people are involved in what we are doing. Anthony was nervous about working with some senior customers of his firm. He had lots of experience meeting with the more junior people, but felt hesitant and unconfident when the meetings involved the heads of departments. For years he had defined his unconfidence issues, "I am not confident with senior people.". You can probably guess what happened when he had to go to those meetings. He projected his unconfidence, which was picked up by the customer and the meetings never went well. When talking with friends about the issue, discussions always seemed to end up with everyone sharing their stories of their own bad meetings, and nothing constructive ever came out of the conversations.

When I talked to Anthony about focusing on his desired outcome rather than the problem, there was an immediate change. He expressed his desired outcome as, "To meet with senior customers while in my Confidence Zone.". When conversations start with, "How can I meet with senior customers while in my Confidence Zone?" instead of, "How can I stop being so unconfident around senior customers?" it changes the focus from the problem to the solution. The discussion goes from negative (how to *stop* something) to positive (how to *create* something). Anthony was then able to focus on all the ways he could *build* his confidence, a very different feeling. This fundamentally changes the nature of the conversation, and builds confidence in the fact that there *is* a solution that will make a difference.

## Mistake 3: Forget to make the desired outcome REALISTIC and ACHIEVABLE

Some of you reading this might be thinking that the desired outcome examples above are not very ambitious. You are right. But they are realistic and achievable for the people concerned. In both cases it was something they could see themselves achieving, so it was motivating for them.

Maria was struggling with her career path at work. When I asked her for her desired outcome she replied, "I want to be a Leadership Team member within five years." Maria had only just joined the company, was 25 years old and was in an administrative assistant position. We had a coaching session and she changed her desired outcome to, " I want a clear plan of the career steps I need to take to get to the Leadership Team, and how to build and develop the skills and experiences I need to take the first step within six months.". Maria realised that just making this simple change in how she phrased her desired outcome had turned her future from being an overwhelming task to an exciting, genuine possibility that she could start planning.

Julia was scared of riding outside the arena with her horse. I asked her what her desired outcome was and she replied, "I am galloping along the beach on my horse, with no saddle or bridle!". Nothing wrong with that as a long-term target, and as a dream to aim for. I truly do believe that if she carries on working the way she is on herself and her horse, she will achieve that desired outcome. However, by having such a huge, far off dream as her target, she actually ended up feeling demotivated whenever she made progress, because however much progress she made it felt tiny compared to where she wanted to be.

So we took that as her 'ultimate dream' and for her desired outcome we broke it down into smaller steps. We started with, "I can ride my horse out by myself at walk trot and canter whilst staying in my Confidence Zone.". She achieved that in just four weeks. Now that was much more motivating. We are now working on another desired outcome which will bring her one step further along the path to her long-term dream.

In both these examples the long-term dream is a great, positive, inspiring vision—definitely something to aim for. However, the further away a dream is, the less clear are the steps to get there and often people end up taking wrong turnings along the way. The desired outcome is a practical, time-focused, realistic achievable outcome we can start working on right away. We know it will bring us closer to our longterm dream, but it's close enough to believe in, and that makes it much more likely to be achieved.

## Mistake 4: Trying to find the 'one right answer'

Most of us, when we have a problem, share it with friends and spend a long time working on it. What we do wrong though, is we try to find the 'one right answer'. So every time anyone comes up with an idea, we look for why it won't work *perfectly*—and move on to examining the next idea. This is a very slow, demoralising, and ineffective way of doing things. Think about it: if you have one thing to try and it doesn't work, how bad do you feel? Pretty bad, because you are right back where you started. How frustrating!

Now, imagine you have twenty things to try, and one of them doesn't work. You still have nineteen others left to try. How much better are you going to feel? How much easier is it going to be to try things, knowing you have many others to try if that one doesn't work out? How much more confident will you be that *one* of those things will help move things forward? Exactly.

Twenty ideas seems like a lot to many of us. However, an interesting thing happens when you come up with twenty options. It turns out that the options you come up with after the tenth one are much better than numbers one to ten. It looks like the first ten mix in our minds and stimulate us to think of better quality ideas.

This is the principle behind the technique of brainstorming that is used in business. The problem is presented (in a useful way, framed as a desired outcome that is realistic and achievable, of course) and then the team bounce ideas off each other. Every idea is written down, without any criticism or judgement. This way, one idea that may seem impossible or even slightly silly, can end up triggering other ideas in people's minds and a lot more useful ideas end up on the list. It is much easier to be creative and imaginative when you know you are going to have fun rather than be criticised, isn't it? One thing to realise is that the worst person for criticising ideas is you. You will know exactly why each idea will not work, or you have tried it before. It doesn't matter. Just write it down and move on to the next idea. After all, you will be the one who chooses what you actually do, so you can afford to write it down, right?

There's also a powerful reason for writing every idea down, even if you disagree with it. An interesting thing happens when you write ideas down, they go into a different part of your brain compared to when you are just listening. When you write things down, you pay attention to them in a different way (it eliminates some of the filters we have for only hearing what we want to hear!), you use different parts of your brain and so, as you are writing them, you will come up with more ideas.

George had come to the coaching session with a very specific issue: his relationship with his partner was deteriorating and he didn't know what to do about it. He had defined the issue as his, and his desired outcome was to have a plan for improving the relationship over the next six months that he could implement while staying in his Confidence Zone. We started brainstorming ideas with a couple of trusted friends of his. As we all offered ideas, first George started doing the 'yes but' we all do inside our heads when people give us ideas. I stopped the exercise and reminded him that he had to write down *every* idea regardless of what he thought of it. Grumbling, he started writing down the ideas he had been negative about. As he wrote the third idea down, he stopped and looked up and said, with some surprise:

"I have just realised that although my first reaction to this idea of 'be nice' sounded stupid, I don't think I am actually very good at saying nice things to my partner. In fact, I tend to be a sarcastic person and can't remember the last time I said something that was just nice…".

In writing down the ideas, George's brain had processed them in a different way to when he was just listening and had opened up an 'Aha!' moment for him that turned out to have a massive impact on his relationship.

## Mistake 5: Going it alone

Sometimes it can be tempting to try and sort things out by yourself. Sometimes it might feel as if you have to, as no one else will understand the issue well enough to help. But one of the biggest mistakes people make when trying to sort out an issue, especially when it involves something as complex as confidence, is trying to go it alone.

First, we need people to make sure we are defining our issue in a useful way. Second, having people to help you check the quality of your desired outcome also helps. Thirdly, having people to brainstorm with really helps to get to the twenty options that will make a significant difference to your strategies. Interestingly, they don't need to know all the ins and outs of the problem or issue. All they need to know is your desired outcome and they can help you brainstorm, which is useful.

Another very important area where having support makes a difference is when it comes to actually acting on some of the ideas your brainstorming came up with. When you have your twenty options, and you choose two or three to try out for the next two to four weeks, it is important to be honest about the support you will need to be able to do these things. Support might be something as simple as having a friend be in the arena when you are riding; or it might be something more like having a colleague give you a small piece of a presentation to do so you can practice your skills knowing you have a safety net. The key is, that the support can be the difference between making progress and not.

Mike was nervous about signing up to a large project his manager, Andrea, had suggested to him. He knew it would be good for his career, but was worried he didn't have the knowledge and experience to do well on it, and didn't want to let the team or himself down. After our brainstorming session, he went and had a conversation with Andrea, and shared his concerns with her. At this meeting he shared his desired outcome and the ideas he had come up with during our brainstorming session. Andrea saw that she could immediately support on two of the options: she authorised Mike going on a training course to update his knowledge in a specific area relevant to the project; and also talked to her peers to get Mike a place on a smaller project that was starting that week so he could build relationships with some key people before the big project started later in the year. This would also give him more detailed experience and insight into how the company ran projects. Andrea was impressed by Mike's work on identifying actions that would make a difference, and in his coming to her to ask for her support in achieving them. The end result was that Mike was very successful in the larger project and credited a large portion of his success to how he had worked to keep everything within his Confidence Zone so he could perform at his best, and to having asked his manager for support.

Another example of this is my friend's experience. She was nervous about traveling her horse in a horse lorry as she had never done this before. She knew she could 'Just do it', but that didn't feel right, it was about a 7 on her Confidence Map and therefore outside her Confidence Zone. I worked with her to identify her desired outcome and some ideas for actions to get her making progress. As a result, we trailered together to a few places, first with me driving so she could see how I did it, then with her driving so I could give her some feedback. We even did a few trips without a horse for practice, and only when she was confident did we consider loading her and travelling her. After a few trips together with her horse, she felt confident about trailering by herself and it was no big deal when she did. The support my friend asked for from me made the whole thing much easier and meant when she did drive by myself she had true confidence based on experience.

So when we have chosen the options we want to try out, we need to make sure we identify the support that will make those options workable, to give us our best chances of success.

## How do we avoid these five mistakes?

These are the five common mistakes people make in business and life when it comes to trying to find solutions to issues that are getting in their way. The good news is that there is a simple way to avoid all 5 of these, and that is to follow a process that highly effective problem solvers in business follow, which I have translated into a simple model for my coaching.

It is called the **IDEAS** model. Because it has five elements to it and those elements spell out **IDEAS**.

**I**: Identify your **I**ssue: your real one, in a useful way.
**D**: Describe your **D**esired outcome: is it realistic, achievable? Something you can control?
**E**: **E**xplore options: I use the word explore deliberately – explore and get 20, without criticism or judgement and write them down.
**A**: Agree **A**ctions: you choose which 2 or 3 options you will do for the next two weeks
**S**: Seek the **S**upport you need: set yourself up for success by making sure you have the support lined up ready!

On the next page there is an example of a real issue where we used this model.

More examples can be found on the Complete Confidence page at cathysirett.com

| STEP: | NOTES: |
|---|---|
| **Identify Issue**<br>Take 5 minutes, and make sure you OWN the issue. | I don't know how to be selected for the best project teams working on the interesting projects (I always end up on the boring admin type tasks!) |
| **Desired Outcome**<br>Take 5 minutes, and make sure the outcome is both realistic and achievable. | I want to be considered for the three new launch team projects coming up in 6 months time, and feel in my Confidence Zone about my ability to do the work AND that I am visible to the people selecting the teams |
| **Explore Options**<br>Take 15 minutes, and write down your options. | 1. Identify the people selecting the teams<br>2. Find out what they are looking for on the teams in people in the role I want<br>3. Look at their previous teams to see who they tend to choose – and talk to them! They might know why<br>4. Identify who they DIDN'T choose in the last projects<br>5. Identify the KNOWLEDGE and SKILLS the team requires<br>6. Do a competency map of the teams and see how I stack up — or not<br>7. Do I know anyone who will give me honest feedback about how I am seen in the company?<br>8. What is MY competency map — the one I think I have, and the one others think I have<br>9. Work out how to fill my competency gaps<br>10. Identify what can I do between now and then to fill those gaps<br>11. Talk to a coach about how I manage the impression I project at work and how I can change that<br>12. Do some psychometric inventories to understand more about myself<br>13. Find a small project I can work on NOW to practice some of these things and prove I am good at them - particularly the pieces people might not have known I can do well<br>14. TALK MORE – hang out at the coffee room, socialise and build those relationships!<br>15. Join the running club (to build relationships)<br>16. Join the next charity day work project (team player)<br>17. Decide WHY I want to be on these project teams — are they right for me or am I doing them because I think I 'should'<br>18. Get involved in a project in my personal life to practice the skills (eg launch of the new junior football team in the village?)<br>19. Read everything I can on product launches and join in every conversation proactively to become more visible as someone who 'gets' launch<br>20. LISTEN: find out what has worked well on previous launch projects and what they plan to do<br>21. THIS time so I can be proactive in the conversations<br>22. BREATHE! |
| **Agree Actions**<br>Choose which 2 to 3 options you will do for the next two weeks. | 1,2,3,5,8 – then replan for the next two weeks |
| **Support Needed**<br>Set yourself up for success by making sure you have the support lined up ready. | Talk to Andrew and Sean for info, get learning to identify and approve the training course, test out Simon, Marie and Bev for feedback... |

## Just one more thing

## Remember to do a reality check

You now have a clear desired outcome, and options for how to get there. Let's just do a reality check that these options and actions are the ones that are really going to make a difference. Find a couple of trusted friends (the ones who will tell you when you have spinach in your teeth before that big meeting) and take them through your Confidence Map and your IDEAS Process. It never hurts to make sure you are still on track on your Confidence Journey as at this stage it is easy to get carried away with the possibilities rather than prioritising the practicalities. Make sure you end up with actions that are achievable, and that will move you closer to your desired outcome and have the support you need to accomplish them.

If you get stuck here, don't worry: there are several Certified Complete Confidence Coaches available to work with you over the phone, the net or face-to-face. You will find their details on cathysirett.com

# CHAPTER 4
## STEP 4: WHAT ABOUT OBSTACLES AND CHALLENGES?

*"There is freedom waiting for you
On the breezes of the sky
And you ask "What if I fall?"
But oh, my darling,
What if you fly?"* — Erin Hanson, Poet

Great! So far on your Confidence Journey you have your 'why', your 'where' you are starting from and your 'how': options that will get you closer to your destination/desired outcome. So we can just get started on our chosen actions and everything will be fine, yes?

Maybe. For some people, just doing the Confidence Map opens their eyes to what is going on to the extent they can walk away and solve things. For others, coming up with the options and getting started makes everything else fall into place. But for some of us, we start on our options and guess what? Stuff happens. On a car journey we can have road works, accidents, and traffic jams that mean we have to change plans. On an ocean trip, where we are often sailing into unknown territory, we can also anticipate challenges and obstacles. In Medieval times on most maps of the world, large uncharted areas were tagged with the writing, "Here be dragons". There were dangerous storms, sea monsters, unexpected reefs and many other dangers for sailors. This can happen on our Confidence Journey as well. How can we plan for these obstacles and challenges that could take our Confidence Journey off course? We can use something called Constructive Negative Visualisation (c). Otherwise known as the 'What if?' Process.

Something we are often told to do when we anticipate obstacles is to 'Think positive' and 'Don't focus on the negative'. This is great advice but when you are scared and anxious it is not always possible. How many times have you been worrying about something ahead and when someone says, "Just visualise the positive", your brain responds with, "Yeah, right!"? A friend of mine was browsing confidence books. She opened one book and on the page in front of her was the statement "Visualise yourself with confidence!". Her instant thought was, "If I could do that I wouldn't have the problem!", and she put the book straight back on the shelf. For many of us when we have confidence concerns, it is impossible for us to imagine things going well, and we are overwhelmed with all the negative possibilities.

Another piece of advice that is often given is to just 'not think about the negatives'. I don't know about you, but my brain doesn't really process 'don't' that well. Tell me, "Don't think about pink elephants." and instantly, I think of pink elephants. In fact, our unconscious mind struggles to relate to negatives: if you say, "Don't bump into the table." it won't hear the 'don't' and more often than not you will bump into the table, again. If you want to have your unconscious mind working with you then one simple step is to never tell it 'not' to do something. All *not* thinking about the negatives does is leave you unprepared for the realities of life, and unsafe. The positive thinkers *do* have a point: if we *over*-focus on the negatives we will not get anywhere—so is there a balance that works?

Yes there is, and that is what Constructive Negative Visualisation is. It is thinking about the possible negatives but in a *constructive* way. Here's how it works, best illustrated with a story I often tell my horse riding clients about my own experience:

I used to be scared of riding in wide open spaces. I would be so nervous I couldn't get on my horse. So I used a good friend of mine as a confidence booster and together we went and played on a large open area. It was great fun and by the end of the day I was feeling very confident. I decided to leave my horse at her house and come back again the next day when she was out at work and ride out on that big area by myself. After all, I was now 'fixed' so it would be fun. The next morning I got up, and took a while to find the clothes I wanted, but I wasn't at all nervous. I couldn't find the car keys and had trouble getting them in the ignition, but I wasn't at all nervous (do you begin to see where this is going?). I drove down to my friend's house and tacked up my horse: funny how all the buckles were really stiff and wouldn't do up properly. I had to redo them several times. But even now I was sure I wasn't nervous. I was humming to myself as I led my horse out onto the wide open space. As we walked out into the open my legs gave way under me and I collapsed in a heap on the ground. Now I had to admit it: I was nervous. My unconscious had been sending me signals since I first got up and I had ignored them. In the end, the only way my unconscious could get me to pay attention and keep me safe (ie stop me from getting on that horse!) was to literally take my legs away from me! I had to laugh as I lay on the ground, realising how much in denial I had been. And I am supposed to know about this stuff!

The interesting thing about this situation, and any situation where our confidence is shaky is that blasting through our own confidence thresholds does not work. If we ignore the subtle signs our unconscious sends us, it will get bigger and shout at us until we *do* listen, so what starts as small butterflies in the stomach, ends up with us shaking and crying at the mere thought of touching our horse, as our brain tries to keep us safe. However, if we listen to the first signals, and respect this message, then we can find ways to move forward and still be safe—and our unconscious will allow us to move forward: *if* it knows we have paid attention to it.

Here's what happened next:

1. The first thing I did was finally acknowledge that I was scared. I wasn't just unconfident, I was terrified. I wasn't sure what I was terrified of, this was something instinctive and almost primeval. A fear that would not let me walk was not something I could ignore anymore. In fact I called my friend on my mobile and told her what had happened. She was actually relieved as usually I appear so confident it was good for her to hear I had fear issues too.

2. The next thing I did was try and work out what I was so scared of: what was the worst thing that could happen? Now this may seem counterintuitive. Most people tell you to visualise the positive and not to focus on the negative things. The trouble is, if your brain is screaming at you to pay attention to the danger, then you really have to take a good look at the danger before your brain will let you even begin to take any positive outcomes seriously. Those negative thoughts do not go away, they are just suppressed, but they are still knocking on the lid trying to get out and will get out just when you least want them to.

3. I decided that the worst that could happen was my horse would bolt off in this huge open space with me helpless on top. I would be out of control. Now part of me laughed at this (if you knew my horse you would realise that the furthest she would bolt would be to the next clump of grass) but I had to take this seriously to move forward. Regardless of what seemed to be common

sense, I was scared of this happening. So I had to find a way to prove to my brain that this was not going to happen before it would let me get on in a calm and confident way.

4. So now I knew the worst that could happen – I could start developing strategies – and combine this with the WHAT IF? Process.

First, I identified my desired outcome: I needed strategies so I could not even get into the situation that my horse would bolt, and I would stay in my Confidence Zone the whole time.

Then I started coming up with options. For each option I ran a WHAT IF? test. Here's how it went:

Option 1: Do groundwork with my horse until she is calm and paying attention to me
   WHAT IF she is not calm? Don't get on
   WHAT IF she *is* calm? Get on

Next option: Get on my horse
   WHAT IF she moves off? Get off and repeat option 1
   WHAT IF she stands calmly? Then move on to the next option

Next option: Ask horse to bend neck to either side calmly
   WHAT IF she doesn't do this? Go back to the previous option
   WHAT IF she *does* do this? Then move on to the next option

Next option: Ask my horse to walk forwards calmly
   WHAT IF she doesn't, or she speeds up? Go back to the previous option and repeat
   WHAT IF she is fine? Enjoy the walk and think about how you are feeling

Next option: Increase speed as desired and both horse and human stay calm

WHAT IF either of us gets tense? Return to the previous option

WHAT IF it goes well? Enjoy the ride!

5. I did one last WHAT IF? test…WHAT IF at *any* time my confidence score went over 5?

Simple. I would return to the previous step and start again!

By following this process all the way through as I lay there on the ground, I was able to reassure my unconscious that I did know what I was doing, that it could trust me, and I was developing strategies that would keep me safe in any situation I could imagine.

## Make sure you KEEP THE CONTRACT

What often happens is we go through this whole process of basically negotiating a contract with our unconscious, to enable us to do something and then, when we start the process, we change our mind. For example, I could have got on my horse, felt fine and ignored all the other things I had thought about and just cantered off—after all I felt great once I was up there. That would be the worst thing I could do! I would be breaking the contract I had made with my unconscious, and proved to it that I could not be trusted to look after my own safety. So next time, well next time it would be *much* harder to reach an agreement, as I had broken the trust this time.

Dieter was concerned with a series of meetings he had coming up with the Leadership Team of his company. It was part of an assessment process for a fast track programme which would make a huge difference to his career. Originally he was scoring himself at an 8 about his first meeting with the Sales Director. He created his Confidence Map and identified that his underlying issue was a fear that he would let himself down by not showing his best. He didn't mind not getting on the programme if he wasn't up to the mark, but not because he had failed to interview well. He had also identified some behaviour patterns that would get in his way: a habit of second guessing his answers often made him appear indecisive, and his quick response to questions sometimes gave the impression he was not thinking things through. He used the IDEAS Process and his desired outcome was to have an interview where he had done his best while staying in his Confidence Zone. The main action that came out of this IDEAS process was to use a notebook to slow himself down and look at to make sure he was staying on topic. He would have a mind map of his planned stories and examples he wanted to share in the interview which was visible, and the opposite page could be used to take notes when the interviewer was talking so he could ensure he was really listening to the questions and not rushing his responses.

When we practiced this, he found this slowed down his responses and gave him confidence he was giving his best answers first, reducing his second guessing habit. We then ran through some Constructive Negative Visualisation:

What if I start second guessing? I will stop and make sure I look at my mind map before responding

What if I start giving answers too quickly and I feel the interviewer things I am not listening well or thinking things through? I will take a breath, and remember to count to three before answering, looking at my notebook to make sure I am responding well

Looks simple, right?

But here's something I have already mentioned: the 5 steps in this Confidence Journey are simple in theory, but not always easy to do in practice. The interview started, and after doing the first 2 steps, Dieter thought it was going so well he stopped following his plan. He just went with his instincts and went well away from the plan he had made. It seemed to be alright: the interview did go well and Dieter made a good impression on the Sales Director. The problem came when he started preparing for his *next* interview which was with the Finance Director. Suddenly his nervousness was back and much worse than before. He couldn't understand it until we talked and he realised that by not sticking to the plan in the first meeting, he had proven to his unconscious that he couldn't be trusted to keep himself 'safe'. His unconscious was now stepping up its game and making him so unconfident he would not be able to do that again. He had not *kept the contract*.

It took some work to resolve this. We *did* resolve it, with some therapeutic coaching, and in his next meeting he stuck to the plan (even when it seemed he could go off plan, he stuck to it) and much to his relief, his nerves stayed away for the rest of the series of interviews. And yes, he did get a place on the programme.

Our unconscious is powerful, and when we work with it, we have to prove we can be trusted. I am sure you can see how the previous steps in the Confidence Journey are prerequisites for *this* step.

Now it is your turn. Think of an activity that, when you visualise yourself doing it, you are at an 8 or 9 on your unconfidence score. Take a look at your Confidence Map for some ideas if you like. Then, with this activity, go through the steps I went through just now:

1. Accept and respect the fact you *are* worried or scared about the activity and it is just your way of keeping yourself safe. Maybe even say thanks to your unconscious for working so hard to keep you alive.

2. Identify what it is that really scares you... there might be more than one thing.

3. Acknowledge the fear that this scary thing 'might' happen.

4. Start the process: identify your desired outcome, remembering the guidelines from that exercise.

5. Identify options and then run the WHAT IF? Process on each option. Keep running options until you feel sure you have covered all the possibilities. This might take a while, but it is a worthwhile investment in your future confidence. Each time you take the time to do this, your unconscious learns that you are trustworthy and will allow you to make the confident choices in future.

6. Do a final, global WHAT IF? Test for WHAT IF your confidence score goes over 5?

This step is invaluable for planning for those scary situations and for using when you are confronted with one. It almost takes longer to read here than it takes to actually do, as I often do it in my head while other people are busy talking!

## Just one more thing

### Everything gets better with practice

Ok, now you need to go and practise this. Remember, you can't expect to get better at something if you don't practise. It's funny, but my painting is still as bad as it was six months ago. I haven't practised, but I did hope! These ways of thinking and building confidence work much better when you practise them until they come easily to you.

# CHAPTER 5
## STEP 5: HOW TO MAKE SURE YOU GET THERE

*"Give me six hours to chop down a tree and I will spend the first four sharpening the axe."* —Abraham Lincoln

A good friend of mine, Kary Oberbrunner once said that many people are, "Bingeing on information and starving on application.". We all know people like this: they research, read, network—but never seem to actually get anything done. That can happen with your Confidence Journey too. When I started working on my own Confidence Journey, I would have my Confidence Map, my options from my IDEAS Process and I would have my WHAT IFs? all worked out. But what happened next? One day I realised that despite my best intentions, nothing had actually changed.

When working on our Confidence Journeys we need to remember it is exactly that: work. What we get out of it will depend on what we put into it. I had let my intentions carry me away and not focused on the implementation.

In this step we focus on making sure your Confidence Journey actually happens so you can reach your destination, your desired outcome.

## How to make things happen

> *"By failing to prepare, you are preparing to fail."* — Benjamin Franklin, Founding Father of the United States of America

> *"A goal without a plan is just a wish."* — Antoine de Saint-Exupery, Writer and Poet

We have all heard the quotes about planning. How important it is, how without it you are likely to drift and not achieve your goal. How do you *feel* about planning?

I think it's a great idea but find it hard to focus on as there are so many more exciting things to do. I have to practically chain myself down to create a spreadsheet for a work project. I don't doubt the *value* of planning, it's just that it's not my first choice of something to focus on. This is the thing about planning; we all know we s*hould* do it but not all of us *like* doing it, even when we know it leads to better results.

So instead of telling you to plan, and leaving it at that, I am going to do exactly what I have done with all the other work in this book: I am going to dig deeper into the whole issue of planning and make sure we find a way that everyone reading this can get the benefits of planning *without* the pain.

When you see the word 'planning', what comes to mind? For many of us the word conjures up images of endless spreadsheets and charts and brings feelings of constraint and boredom. No wonder we don't want to do it. For others, who enjoy that level of detail the danger is they get so lost in the planning that nothing actually gets done; the plans are superb but the outcomes? Not so much! The key with planning and implementation is to find a way that works for *you*. And what works for you might be very different from what works for your colleague, your sibling, your friends or anyone else. This can make it challenging when we are building a plan for our Confidence Journey, because sometimes our friends will have their own ideas, based on what works for them and we have to stand our ground and make sure we are doing what works for us. So what are the options?

In this chapter I share with you four ways of planning that have had great results for many different types of people. You will find one will resonate more with you than others, or you may find that a hybrid of two approaches makes sense to you. That's ok! Find the approach that feels good for you and how you like to work and use that to make your Confidence Journey happen.

To help you decide, there are some examples of the different planning approaches on the website.

## 1. Spreadsheet Steve

Steve loved managing projects. It was his job and he was good at it. He could convert his team's creative ideas into concrete plans and they invariably happened. When he hit a confidence roadblock, he built his Confidence Journey and the logical way to plan it for him was to create a spreadsheet-based project plan. Like any project, his spreadsheet had weeks along the top, and his chosen activities from his IDEAS Process down the left-hand side. He then decided what order he would do his activities in and blocked in the details week by week, allowing for how much time he knew he had to work on things, until they were all done. He also broke down his planned activities into smaller chunks so, for example, some parts could be done in week 3, some in week 5. With his project management background he found it easy to work out how all the activities interlinked and would fit together to lead to results.

He then used a red/amber/green colour coding of each cell in the spreadsheet to show which things had not been done yet, which had been started but weren't complete, and which had been finished. For Steve, this was the best way to make sure his Confidence Journey happened and fitted perfectly with his style and his experience. For him, this was the easy way to plan

When his partner Melanie saw his spreadsheet she was horrified. She had been working on building her own Confidence Journey related to a family issue and was ready to plan her actions to make it happen, but one look at Steve's spreadsheet and she was ready to give up. For her it was too complex, too detailed and was not something she wanted to do. Melanie found a different way to plan her Confidence Journey.

## 2. Map Melanie

Melanie was a creative director in an advertising agency. Her job was coming up with ideas, and working with others to share those ideas with clients and co-workers. For her, spreadsheets were something the finance team used, not creative people. For Melanie, the effective way to plan was to use MindMaps. After all she used them at work and found them easy to use. Adding a few tweaks turned them from a way to capture ideas to an effective way to plan the implementation of IDEAS. Mind maps are used by a lot of people and are quite straightforward to set up. She had a large piece of paper and in the centre wrote her desired outcome. From that circle she then put lines leading to other circles, each of which contained one of the actions she had chosen to focus on. For these action circles she had then broken the actions down into smaller steps and these were in smaller circles around the action circle. From this map, she then identified the daily and weekly tasks she would do to achieve each action and, ultimately, her desired outcome. This is a very visual way of tracking progress, and very different from the tables and boxes of the spreadsheet approach.

For Melanie this worked well and kept her on track to her results. Her colleague Graham looked at her map and wondered how on earth she could tell what she was doing next—he needed something more structured, but, like Melanie, he was a highly visual person and also knew a spreadsheet wouldn't work for him.

## 3. Graphic Graham

Graham was working on a Confidence Journey to overcome the nerves that had started getting in the way of his enjoyment of his passion: car racing. He was looking forward to getting back to the state of carefree happiness he had before his recent accident. One of the challenges Graham had with making his Confidence Journey happen was that he also had a very high pressure job, and he often lost sight of the importance of his desired outcome under the weight of everything else he was doing. It was hard to keep his Confidence Journey front of mind and prioritised during the week and he often reached a weekend having done nothing to work on his confidence. He was starting to feel bad about his lack of progress until we had a conversation where we explored graphic visualisation.

There are several styles of graphic visualisation but they all have some common factors.

First, you create an inspiring visual of your desired state. You can be creative, be colourful and include everything you want your desired state to include. Graham really went to town on this and produced a powerful visual of himself in his car grinning like a madman and thoroughly enjoying the drive, surrounded by his cheering family and friends and with a small image of drinks to celebrate afterwards. This picture becomes the anchor for the plan: it is posted on the wall where you can see it every day and reminds you constantly of the positive, exciting outcome that you are moving towards *if* you do the work.

Next, all you do is add pieces of paper in front of this picture representing months or weeks, and on these write down what needs to be done in those months or weeks. For Graham, weeks worked better and he had about 12 sheets of A4 on the wall in front of his picture with actions for each week. His family wasn't too happy about having one of their living room walls taken up with this plan, so he photographed the whole thing and kept it on his phone. He did keep one page up on the back of the door, where he saw it in the morning when he first got up: the desired outcome picture as that would make sure he kept his goal front of mind and prioritised every day. Graham was someone excited by the vision of what he was moving towards, and keeping that in sight motivated him to do the tasks he knew would get him there.

For his son, William, who was struggling with confidence to speak up in his classes at college, and getting low marks as a result, this didn't work. However bright and exciting his picture of success, it just didn't seem to motivate him to action at all. This was because William needed a different approach. For William, the picture that kept him motivated was one he drew of what would happen if he *didn't* work on his confidence.

Some people are 'move towards' people and are motivated by making progress towards a better state. Some however are more strongly motivated by 'moving away from' a negative state. Most of us are a mix of the two so for the most powerful Graphic Visualisation I recommend creating one picture of where you don't want to end up—and one of where you do. That way you have the best of both worlds!

I have been coaching confidence for 25 years and when I finally decided to write this book bringing everything together I knew that motivation to do the actual day-to-day effort of writing and editing would be hard at times. So I created my two pictures: one was of lots of confident people waving copies of the book in the air and celebrating how it had helped them. The other picture was of me, sitting alone and isolated and not impacting anyone because I had not finished the book. Every day I would look at both pictures. Depending on the day, one or other would inspire me to actually sit down and get on with this writing.

However, both I and another client of mine found the linear planning element of the graphic visualisation a bit restricting—and decided to use the pictures but add another element.

## 4. Building Blocks Bernadette

Bernadette was a successful endurance rider, on her way to the top of that sport with her lovely horse Lily. Unfortunately, on a couple of recent rides Bernadette had experienced some falls which had left her tense and worried when riding, and this was affecting her horse. So much so that they were not finishing races, and the nerves were getting worse.

Bernadette undertook the Confidence Journey steps and diligently worked through them. She identified that her fear came from her realisation that although she had ridden since she was a child, she didn't really understand the underlying principles of horse behaviour, horse psychology and horse riding enough. She had what we call 'Mechanical confidence' where she had learned to ride by following the mechanical rules of riding, rather than the 'authentic confidence' that came from a broad and deep awareness of core principles.

When it came to her IDEAS exercise she had a lot of things she could do: some were knowledge based, some were skills building and some were about creating positive experiences and trust with her horse, with whom she had never really established a connected relationship. Now it was time to make a plan and while she was happy creating the motivating pictures, both the 'moving towards' and the 'moving away from', she was struggling to map the tasks and activities out into weeks on the timeline.

"It just feels too restrictive.", she said. "I mean, if I am building a relationship with Lily, then what I do each week has to depend to some extent on where she is on any given day, so I can't make a plan because it might have to change, in fact it most likely *will* change!".

Bernadette had identified a very common challenge in planning, particularly when other people or living beings are involved over whom we have no direct control. We can make *our* plan but it might not fit in with theirs. In these cases, the Building Blocks approach can be invaluable.

Bernadette wrote each of her tasks and activities onto a separate sticky note, and placed them on the timeline where she thought they were *most likely* to happen. However, she set herself the goal that each week she would do three things that made progress towards her goal. It didn't matter which three, just three things. She could move the sticky notes each week to reflect the reality of what was happening. This way she could keep sight of her goal, still make progress and yet build in the flexibility she needed because she was working with a living creature who had her own ideas, moods and challenges.

This approach of using graphic visualisation combined with Building Blocks can be very powerful when your Confidence Journey involves other people or things outside your direct control.

## Just one more thing

## KISS your planning

There is an acronym often used in the corporate world: KISS. Keep it Simple, Stupid. First heard in the US Navy in the 1960s it was used as a design principle to ensure that things weren't over complicated. If there was a simpler way of doing something, or designing something—that would have priority over anything more complex. Or you can think about the philosophical concept of Occam's razor: If there exist two explanations for an occurrence the simpler one is usually better. Another way of saying it is that the more assumptions you have to make, the more unlikely an explanation. What this means for us is that when we are deciding which approach would work for us in making our Confidence Journey happen, the simpler we can make it, the more likely it will be to actually happen. For some of us, our plan could be as simple as writing tasks in our diary and doing them—it *can* be that simple. Find the way that works for *you*.

Remember, it's the *outcome* of the plan that matters, not the time spent making the plan itself!

Congratulations! You now know how to build your own Confidence Journey. On the website, cathysirett.com you will find a free downloadable workbook containing all the worksheets for your Confidence Journey, free to everyone who has bought this book. There are also lots of examples along with some extra podcasts and vlogs. Please feel free to head over there and discover resources that will help you along your way.

Now, let's explore the rest of the book.

In the next section, Part 2, I share some key ways to expand your Confidence Zone. These chapters will give you lots of insights and new ways of thinking that will add value to your IDEAS Process and increase the actions and options you come up with.

In Part 3 you will find some of the traps that people can fall into while on their Confidence Journeys, as well as tips to avoid these traps and accelerate your progress.

Part 4 shares the seven golden rules of how to help someone else on their Confidence Journey. Once we know how to be confident ourselves it can be really difficult to watch others struggle. How can we help in a way that makes a real difference to them?

Part 5, the last part of this book will show how we *stay* confident, so instead of being a one-off process we use for one issue at a time, we can build up our capability to be our own Confidence Coaches now and into the future.

Enjoy!

# PART 2
## EXPANDING YOUR CONFIDENCE ZONE

In this part of the book you will find the information and insights you need to expand your Confidence Zone. These are the main elements I use in my coaching when I work with people to help them get the most out of their Confidence Journey. In the following chapters you will learn ways of thinking and tools that will help make you your own best Confidence Coach

# CHAPTER 6
## HOW TO STOP GETTING IN YOUR OWN WAY

*"Your worst enemy cannot harm you as much as your own unguarded thoughts."* —Buddha

It was one of my first meetings with fellow coach and entrepreneur Vicky. She had a lovely set up with her work office in a purpose built studio at the bottom of her garden, fully equipped and with a separate room for her coaching sessions. She had coached a lot in her life, including on some advanced programmes in top flight organisations, and yet, for some reason, she wasn't coaching now.

During our own coaching session, I noticed that we seemed to be going round in circles. Every time I thought we were making progress towards her getting back into coaching, something else would come up in the conversation and we would be back to how impossible it was. Her husband had a high powered job, he travelled a lot, she had to host business meetings, etc.

Our session had been a long one and it was time I went. As I put on my jacket and got ready to leave, I looked at her and asked her a question that had been sitting in the back of my mind for the last few minutes:

"How are you getting in your own way?". She looked puzzled, and I left, wondering if I would ever see her again.

A few weeks later she called me. She said that question had been going round her head since the moment she heard it. She realised she *had* been getting in her own way and now had started dealing with it. Within weeks she had her first clients at her home office, we were working together on some corporate business, became friends and are still friends today. That one question enabled her to expand her Confidence Zone *so* much. What had been happening was that she had been allowing a whole series of limiting beliefs to get between her and her goal. That's what this chapter is about: how to deal with limiting beliefs.

We all have limiting beliefs. These are beliefs that limit what we do or say and even think.

Some of them are useful. For example, my limiting belief that I will burn myself if I put my hand in a fire stops me getting burned. My limiting belief that I am not a good enough rider to ride an unknown four-year old eventing horse around a cross country course—well *that* keeps me safe.

Our whole world, our whole reality, everything we choose to do and say and how we do and say it is all based on the beliefs we have about ourselves and the world. The question is how *useful* are the beliefs we hold when it comes to helping us enjoy our lives?

As I have already suggested, many of these beliefs are there because they were useful at some stage in our life and many of them will continue to be useful. My belief that it matters if I am polite to people is very useful as my work involves working with lots of people. However, there are times when these beliefs can end up being the opposite of useful, and can actually get in the way of what we want to do with our lives.

One client I worked with recently, Shona, held a strong belief about her horse riding, "I can't jump!". While this belief had done a great job of keeping her safe when riding, she was now feeling frustrated by it. She would go out for long rides with friends and when they were happily jumping over small logs and having fun doing it, she ran into the belief that she couldn't jump and was unable to join in. The few times she had tried to join in, she had been so tense the jump had gone badly wrong—confirming her belief that she couldn't jump.

This is one reason limiting beliefs matter—if you hold a limiting belief and try to go against it you are fighting yourself and end up putting yourself in a physically, emotionally or mentally damaging situation. If you have a belief that you can't jump and then point yourself at a jump your unconscious, whose job is to preserve your 'self' (remember, it's programmed to protect and preserve your belief structure) will kick into action and can actually make sure the event goes wrong. You will suddenly tense up, or 'forget' to get into the right position, or hold the reins too tightly. This is your unconscious simply working hard to preserve your belief structure. In some cases, you might do the jump just fine, and breathe a huge sigh of relief when you have done it, but your unconscious will realise you just went against one of your beliefs, and so the next time you think about jumping, your unconscious will cause you to feel even more unconfident, keeping you safe and on the ground.

It is often useful at this stage to write down 10-20 beliefs that are currently impacting your life—and see how many of them fit into the category of being *limiting* beliefs. Most of us will have beliefs about how good we are, how safe we are, how much we know, how nice we are—anything that affects how you go about your life can be a limiting belief. Then next to each belief, write down what is useful about that belief.

As an example, here are some from some of the conversations I have had with clients:

**Belief**: *I can't ski well.* **Usefulness**: *Keeps me safe! I don't put myself in dangerous situations.*

**Belief**: *I am not a runner.* **Usefulness**: *This means I avoid running in front of other people so they can't criticise me.*

**Belief**: *I have never been a good presenter.* **Usefulness**: *Stops me from signing up for making presentations so I can never look a fool in front of my colleagues.*

**Belief**: *Other people always know more than me.* **Usefulness**: *Makes me think very carefully before I speak up in meetings so I never look stupid.*

One thing you will notice as you do this exercise, is that you will start to feel differently about some of these beliefs. For some of them you will nod and say, "That's a useful belief", and you will decide to keep those. Others, you will look at and say to yourself, "Well, that's just stupid!" or, "That's a bit weird!" or, "That's crazy and not at all useful!". Knowing this, you can now take those latter beliefs and think about how to turn them into something more useful to you.

Let's look at the beliefs from earlier and see how doing this can change things:

**Belief**: *I can't jump.* **Usefulness**: *Keeps me safe! I don't put myself in dangerous situations.*

So this belief is pretty useful-—being safe is important. However, the black and white nature of this belief means I will *never* be able to jump. That's certainly not useful as I would like to be jumping out on rides with my friends and at some stage do small showjumping courses too. How can this belief be reworded so it still keeps me safe but is also useful in helping me achieve my goals?

How about I say, "I can't jump—yet."?

Adding the word 'yet' to a limiting belief reminds us that we are dynamic beings capable of growth and development, which sometimes our unconscious mind forgets. Our unconscious mind is very quick to learn some things—and very slow and reluctant to change that view once learned. Just adding the word 'yet' to a limiting belief changes the belief from something that limits us to something that could potentially empower us.

One of my friends, Evelyn, told me many times that she was no good with computers and she didn't understand them. I realised I was hearing limiting beliefs, and mentally added the word 'yet' to each of them. Then I asked her, "Has anyone ever taught you *how* to use a computer?". She stopped in her tracks and looked surprised as she thought about it.

"No, now you come to mention it, I have never had a lesson, or had anyone show me…".

When we had identified that as the issue, we were able to use the IDEAS Process from Step 3 of the Confidence Journey to find lots of ways to change her situation and now she confidently uses her laptop and the software to master her role as a teacher.

One thing here we did not change her belief to, "I am good with computers," or ask her to positively visualise being good. Even just typing that now I know her unconscious would be going, "Yeah, right!" as that belief is not 'believable' to her! What we did change the belief to was, "I can be good enough at computers when I have learned about them.". When Evelyn read that belief out loud, her unconscious voice said, "Ok, I can believe that!" and so now her beliefs are working *with* her rather than *against* her.

Now some of the limiting beliefs we write down won't work with this approach so let's dig a bit deeper and we will find a way of expanding our Confidence Zone beyond other limiting beliefs that can't be resolved by using the 'yet' technique.

Fundamentally, everything we think, believe or do has a positive intent for us (which it must have as otherwise we would not hold onto it, right?). It goes back to the positive intent of our unconscious mind in general, which is to keep us safe. When we think of safety, we tend to focus on physical safety. This is the primary safety that comes to mind first. An example of how our unconscious helps us with this is if we sprain an ankle, or pull a muscle we then consciously adapt our movements to avoid hurting ourselves. However, after a very short while we do this unconsciously as our unconscious mind takes over, stops us putting weight on our sprained ankle and keeps us from hurting ourselves.

Very useful! However, the unconscious isn't quite as good at *stopping* the taking care process. Many people discover that months after their ankle has healed they are still not putting weight on it normally. Many of us end up with other aches and pains as a result of not walking 'normally' to avoid hurting our pulled muscle even though that pulled muscle healed up ages ago. This is an example of how the positive intent of our unconscious can lead to not so positive outcomes. This is something it is important to realise—just because something has a negative effect, doesn't mean it didn't have a positive intent.

What about these limiting beliefs? Well, some of them help keep us physically safe. For example, I have a limiting belief that I can't ride well enough (yet) to ride a top-level cross country course. By believing this, I make sure I don't try it and so avoid falling off or having an accident. Clearly a positive intent.

If some limiting beliefs keep us from physical harm, what about the others? I mean, how can the limiting belief, "I am useless at drawing.", have anything to do with staying safe?

Well, as we have all experienced, pain isn't just physical. It can be emotional too. For example, disappointment is often painful. So, if I were to do a drawing and be disappointed when it turns out badly (or just less than perfect) that disappointment could really upset me. My unconscious might then decide to keep me safe from that pain by giving me a limiting belief to make sure I avoided drawing again, thus staying safe from that emotional pain or disturbance. In fact this was what was happening to Caroline. She had always enjoyed art, but after repeatedly being told that there was no point doing art unless you were going to 'be the best', she had gradually stopped drawing. Even though on the rare occasions she *did* draw she found the process enjoyable and fulfilling, it was the thinking about doing it that was upsetting. She woke up one day and realised it had been several years since she had drawn anything, and when she thought about drawing again a voice in her head whispered, "Well it won't be any good anyway, so don't bother.". Her unconscious used that limiting belief to keep her safe. Quite often, emotional pain can be from patterns that are imposed on us in our childhood. If we grow up learning that anything not perfect is not worth doing then when we produce something less than perfect, we 'run' that pattern, feel upset and even unworthy. Then of course, we are in emotional pain and yes, you guessed it, our unconscious steps in to prevent that happening again.

A third level of pain isn't really a pain, but it's a threat. Since our unconscious is so concerned about protecting us, it might be worth thinking for a moment about what 'us' our unconscious is protecting. If I believe in myself as a competent, worthy person who is good at most things, then to do anything that threatens this belief could be upsetting. Therefore my unconscious might stop me from doing anything I might not be good at. Again we can see a positive intent to preserve my identity, my sense of self as a competent person. However, the outcome could be that I never try anything new and never take the kind of risks that could lead to greater happiness further down the line.

Limiting beliefs are tools our unconscious uses to protect us physically, emotionally and mentally, and to preserve our sense of 'self'. So one of the first things to do when you look at all the limiting beliefs you have is to identify: what is the positive intent of this limiting belief?

Sometimes just doing this causes that limiting belief to collapse. I worked with someone recently who had a limiting belief that because she had started skiing late, she would never be a good skier. We identified that one positive intent of this belief was to stop her from being upset by negatively comparing herself with more experienced friends who had skied for years. When she realised it was actually a belief that had been useful in her early days but no longer really mattered, as she didn't really care what other skiers thought about her any more, it literally disappeared from her beliefs in that instant.

Even if the belief doesn't collapse, identifying the positive intent can be very useful because, once you have identified it you can:

- Decide if that positive intent is still *relevant* (it might date from childhood and you now have adult resources to apply to the situation).
- Decide that you can achieve that positive intent in a *different* way, without the limiting belief.

Often, these two steps are also enough to 'collapse' a limiting belief.

An example of this was Joshua who came to me not knowing why he wasn't being promoted at work. We uncovered a limiting belief he hadn't realised he held which was, "It's wrong to boast about yourself.". Now the positive intent of this belief is clearly that he doesn't come across as arrogant and big-headed. When he was growing up these were the two worst things his father could say about someone. When his father declared someone as arrogant or big-headed that was the end of the friendship or relationship. In fact at work Joshua was known to be a great co-worker, collaborative, always generous in sharing credit on projects and he was widely admired and respected. As we explored this belief, and asked, "How does it *not* help you?" Joshua realised how much holding onto this belief was actually getting in his way at work, preventing him from doing well in the interviews and assessment centres required for promotion.

How could we keep the positive intent of the limiting belief—and help Joshua get out of his own way at the same time? We created a desired outcome of achieving this and ran the IDEAS Process from Step 3 of the Confidence Journey. The result was an action to explore how other people Joshua admired did get promoted and do well in interviews *without* being seen as arrogant and big-headed. Joshua discovered that they all used what we call a 'fact-based' approach: that is they described actual examples of things they had done, in a factual way. Doing this meant that they could present their successes and good performance points without being seen as anything other than simply sharing what had happened in a pragmatic way. Joshua practised this and found it worked well and yes, he did get that next promotion.

So if we ask the limiting belief how we can achieve those positive outcomes while still keeping the positive intent of the limiting belief, and apply the IDEAS Process, we can find ways to achieve our desired outcome and we can get out of our own way.

## Just one more thing

## What if you become too attached to your limiting belief?

I heard someone describing themselves to a friend the other day. They started off with the usual: height, a joke about weight, their job and their hobbies. This is how the conversation went.

Julia: "Oh and I am very stressy person! Especially when I am driving! I get all tense and am a road rage driver!". She laughed as she said this.

Friend: "You know, you can do things that will make your driving much less stressful…".

Julia: "Really? Because I always end up with a stiff neck and shoulders after driving!".

Friend: "Yes! You can get an instructor/observer from the Institute of Advanced Motorists to come out and drive with you and they can help you be more relaxed…".

Julia: "Oh I wouldn't like anyone sitting next to me while I was driving. I am so stressy it would be embarrassing!".

Friend: "Well, it would take away that tension, and you could reach the end of your drive relaxed and smiling instead of tense and worried…".

Julia thought for a moment. I could see the possibility of being relaxed about driving going through her mind. Then she sighed, shook her head and said,

"It wouldn't work. I am a lost cause!".

This is an example of where an initial belief has become so strongly attached to identity that the person refuses to change it, even when it is clear that changing it would have a huge impact on the quality of their daily life.

Now some of you reading might be going, "How crazy!", "How irrational!". Others might be thinking, "Oh my goodness, I have some beliefs like that...". In some ways this person's insistence on her identity as 'a stress driver' is quite logical. After all, her experience has been that she gets stressed when she drives and people criticise her for it. So if she cannot work out how to change it, what other reason can there be for it? She must just be a stressy person, otherwise she would have changed it.

This is a perfect example of how a limiting belief, especially one that we don't have the resources, knowledge, information or support to change, can become so strongly attached to our identity, our vision of who we are, that we make it impossible for ourselves to accept support and help even when it is offered.

How can you spot a limiting belief that is getting close to becoming attached to your identity?

One way is to listen carefully when you talk about yourself. Listen for when you describe yourself as 'being' something, when, in fact, you are just 'doing' something; when you say you 'are' something, rather than you 'behave as' something.

For example, if I say, "I am an unconfident person.", that is a statement of identity. By the way it's highly likely to be untrue. After all, *everyone* is confident in something. If you think you are an 'unconfident person' then how do you get dressed each day? How do you decide what to eat? See, you are confident in some things. Everyone is.

If I say, "I behave in an unconfident way in *these* situations...", now I am describing a behaviour. The great thing is that I can *choose* my behaviour (most of the time, anyway!). I can even take it a step further and change the words I use. If I am unconfident in situations where I don't know much about the subject, I can just say, "In these situations, where I don't know much about the subject, I am quieter and speak less.".

If we look at that last sentence, we can see that we are being more specific, more useful. Instead of calling myself an unconfident person, which is going to take a *lot* of effort to fix, I can now see that where I do not know much about the situation I tend to be quieter and speak less and you know, in my eyes there is nothing wrong with that. I have gone from labelling myself as something undesirable and unpleasant (i.e. unconfident) and something I need to 'fix' to simply describing a perfectly acceptable behaviour. How interesting.

Why does this matter? When a limiting belief becomes attached to your identity, you lose control over that belief. You lose the choice over who you are and how you behave. You give up your chance to become anyone different. This is fine if you are totally happy with who you are and how you are.

Here is a question to think about—how do you describe yourself?

What limiting beliefs are in *your* description of yourself?

How can you change how you word those beliefs so they represent a behaviour you can choose, rather than represent something you need to 'fix' about yourself?


For more examples of how to stop getting in your own way, go to cathysirett.com and take a look at the resources in the Complete Confidence section.

# CHAPTER 7
## HOW TO SWITCH ON CONFIDENCE IN THOSE MOMENTS WHEN YOU NEED IT

*"The world as we have created it is a process of our thinking. It cannot be changed without changing our thinking."* — Albert Einstein

How amazing would it be if, in a moment when you were anxious or concerned, you could just turn a switch and be flooded with feelings of confidence and competence? That would be wonderful, wouldn't it?

Here's the good news—there is a proven technique for achieving this. It is used by public speakers, TV hosts, and athletes all around the world. It is also used by people like you and me, people who just want to build a big enough Confidence Zone to enjoy our lives and not get derailed by challenging moments. The technique is called *anchoring*.

The thing is that we are already anchoring. It's a natural process that happens to all of us. Have you ever caught a scent in the air and it has taken you back to a childhood memory?

Have you ever been somewhere and it reminds you so much of a memory that you experience all the feelings of that memory as if it were today? Sometimes we experience the feelings and can't even remember the details of the memory, just the way it felt. That's anchoring—and it's when feelings, emotions and memories get attached to an anchor of a smell, a taste, a sound, a sight or a feeling.

Most of these anchors happen unconsciously. We experience happiness and at that moment the scent of a certain flower wafts past us. The next time we smell that flower we are back in that moment of happiness. We also create negative anchors naturally. I once ate some tinned peaches, then coincidentally had a stomach upset, and still to this day cannot even think of eating tinned peaches without feeling ill!

The good news is that we can also create our own anchors consciously. This means we can choose the feelings we want to recall, and we can choose the anchor.

The easiest way to build an anchor is to do it when something great is actually happening. When I was cave diving in Florida, the last ten minutes of every dive was swimming about a foot underwater in the hot springs full of plant and fish life whilst able to see the snow and ice above water. The feeling of having had a successful dive, of having accomplished that morning's challenge filled my heart and all my senses were fully engaged. One morning, while on this swim back to the centre, I realised this would be a wonderful 'state' to anchor. If I could make it so I could access this wonderful emotional state at will, that would be a powerful tool to have.

On the next dive I warned my partner that I would be a bit longer than usual on the 'swim home' section so she wouldn't worry. We had a challenging dive (I had to remove my tanks and scramble through a narrow tunnel while underwater in a cave, the first time I had ever done that!) which had gone well and I was feeling accomplished, resourceful and happy. So while I was swimming along I went through the anchoring process which has 6 steps:

1. *Decide on the physical 'trigger' for your anchor.* I chose touching my left first knuckle with my right index finger. It's not something I do often so I would be unlikely to trigger the anchor accidentally, and yet it was also something I could do discreetly in a meeting if I needed to.
2. *Hold the trigger while IN the actual state.* While kicking along, I had my finger on my knuckle, pressing down a bit to make sure I could feel it.
3. *Fully experience the moment and state as intensely as possible* (whilst holding the trigger!). For this step I focused on paying attention to each of my five senses for a full minute.

   First I focused on what I could hear (the sound of my breathing through the SCUBA gear, and the water around me).

   Then I focused on what I could smell (yes, you can smell things underwater—I could smell the water, my own breath...).

   Next it was what I could taste (those of you who have Scuba dived know that there is a distinct taste of the mouthpiece and the air you are breathing).

   Then I focused on the sense that is strongest for me—what I was feeling (the warmth of the water, the sensation of it against me as I moved through it, the wetsuit against my skin).

   Finally I focused on what I was seeing (the amazingly bright colours of the plants and fish, the sunlight patterns as they came through the water, the snow above the water and the stunning blue sky through the ripples and bubbles from my swimming). You can probably tell I still recall this moment quite intensely!

4. *At the instant you are experiencing the moment at its highest intensity—BREAK your trigger.* After going through each of the five senses I then tried to just fully be in the moment and felt emotions rising inside me. At that moment I took my finger away from my knuckle before any sensation could fade, so I made sure that the trigger was set for that peak of feeling.

5. *Break state.* I had to come out of the state I was in, so I thought about what I would be doing later that evening and the emails I would have to write for work, that was definitely a state change

6. *Test the trigger.* I then made sure the anchoring process had worked. I stopped moving for a moment, touched my finger to my knuckle, and instantly felt all the feelings and sensations I had anchored there—great! If the response had been weak or vague I would have gone through the process again one or two more times to really make sure the anchor was properly set.

This was all done about 15 years ago and yet today as I touch that knuckle with that finger, a smile spreads across my face and I am back inside that moment, with access to all the feelings and sensations. How wonderful is that?

This anchor has been invaluable when I have been in meetings where I am being challenged or feel threatened. Triggering this anchor restores my emotional state and I can respond intelligently and from a positive place rather than reacting in fear or out of anxiety. It definitely enables me to expand my Confidence Zone.

## Why do anchors work?

What is great about anchors is we know the science behind them. It all starts with the Russian scientist Pavlov who found that by linking two unrelated things, you can actually make them connect. For him it was linking the sound of a bell with the arrival of food. Since the arrival of food caused salivation it was easy to prove that eventually just the sound of the bell triggered the emotional state that was present when food was expected.

In neuroscience terms what happens is that when two nerve cells (neurons) repeatedly fire at the same time, they actually grow physical connections so firing one will then automatically trigger the other neuron to fire. What is even better is that neurons fire whether we are doing something—or whether we are remembering it, which means we can build anchors from memories. Doing this takes a bit more effort than if you can capture the actual moment, but still results in powerful anchors that give you access to emotional states whenever you want.

The easiest way to create an anchor from a memory is to work with a colleague or friend as they can coach you through the process, which is similar to the one above with just a few tweaks.

1. *Choose your physical trigger.*

2. *Remember the feeling/state you want to anchor.*

3. *Immerse yourself IN that feeling.* For this to work effectively you have to be *inside* the feeling, not an observer looking from the outside.

4. *Have your friend coach you through your five senses* by asking you what can you smell? What else? What can you taste? What else? And have them take notes of what you say.

5. *Have your friend coach you through intensifying the state.* They do this by taking what you have said you are experiencing for each sense and then asking you to intensify each experience. For example when they get to remember what you can see, they can say, "Now, make the colours richer, bring more saturation to them.". On each sense they can coach you to *intensify* what you are

experiencing. There is an example of this process on the website cathysirett.com.

6. *As you feel your experience of the memory reaching peak intensity—BREAK the trigger.*

7. *Now tell your friend what you had for breakfast* (this is a good way to break state).

8. *Test the anchor:* how well does it work? When working with memories you may need to repeat the setting process a couple of times.

Congratulations! You now know how to set an anchor from a memory.

There is one more way you can set an anchor, but you need an experienced coach to work with you on this one. An experienced coach can create the emotional state you are wanting to anchor with skilful questioning and then guide you to anchoring it. However, this is a specialist skill, so make sure your coach is competent before investing time with them.

There are some additional notes for this and some examples in the Complete Confidence section at cathysirett.com. You can also find an audio track that will talk you through the process which you can use if you are by yourself and want to set an anchor for something.

## Just one more thing

### Anchors aren't the answer to everything

There are some things to consider before setting your anchors. They won't solve every confidence problem or challenge you have! If you need a boost to get started, or a kick of confidence or resourcefulness to buy you time then anchors are ideal. What they are not so good for is if you have a deep underlying fear of a situation.

For example, if you have a fear of heights and are planning to go on a high ropes course don't use anchors to get you up there because guess what? Anchors don't last forever, emotional states wear off and you could find yourself up a tree without your confidence which would not be a good thing.

For the deeper fears and anxieties, the Confidence Journey is more effective. Anchors are a tool we can add for bursts of confidence and resourcefulness when we need them.

Here are some examples of where people have used anchors effectively to expand their Confidence Zone:

- To overcome nerves walking on stage to do a keynote speech knowing that once they got going they would be fine.
- To handle a moment of conflict in a meeting in which they were confident of their value and material.
- To deal with an emotional reaction to an external anchor (a smell, noise or phrase) to regain control of one's self.
- To reset a positive emotional state after a stressful event.
- To create a state change between, for example, work and home life.

The states they have anchored include confidence, resourcefulness, calm, relaxed, unstressed, ready for anything, creative flow, focused thinking, attention to detail, patience, enthusiasm, energy, listening, feeling capable—and many more.

Where can *you* use anchors to expand your Confidence Zone?

# CHAPTER 8
## HOW TO NEGOTIATE WITH CONFIDENCE KIDNAPPERS

*"You don't have to hold yourself hostage to who you used to be."* — Oprah Winfrey

Many times in this book we have said that lack of confidence is just our unconscious keeping us safe. How much of our day-to-day staying safe habits are things we have on autopilot—crossing the road, not eating food when it's too hot, picking up a vibe about an unsafe situation? How great is that? If we had to consciously think about everything we do every day to stay safe I am sure we would go mad with too much stuff in our heads, so our unconscious is doing a very useful, very helpful job. If it didn't do this, then we would be spending so much time thinking about these things we would not be able to do anything else! So our unconscious has an unconditionally positive intent: it is always trying to help us.

Fortunately it is very good at this.

Unfortunately, because most of us don't know this is going on, we don't realise that the unconscious needs to be told when things change and it doesn't need to protect us anymore. I know people who years after spraining an ankle, still won't use that leg first when climbing stairs. In physical therapy, there are many people who have twisted bodies, sore muscles from years of compensating for a broken bone that healed within eight weeks. But their unconscious is still causing them to move in ways to avoid hurting that broken bone and avoid the pain. Post-injury physiotherapy is useful partly because it reprograms the body to work properly again after the original injury heals.

Let's say we love horses. Let's also say that we are a bit nervous about them. If every time we get on our horse we are nervous, what is our unconscious going to think? It is going to think, "Well, if you are nervous of doing this, let me keep you safe from that feeling. Let me stop you from getting on at all, then you won't have to deal with this.".

This is why you find yourself going out to your horses and by the time you have cleaned up the field and yard and groomed your horses it turns out there isn't really time to ride. Let's say that on this day you have to get back to pick the children up from school. So your conscious mind says, "Let's get our partner to take the children out for the day, then I won't have to worry about that," and we go to the yard, clean up, groom and then notice that the feed room really needs reorganising. Our unconscious is helping us to not be worried, helping us to not be nervous by keeping us busy noticing other things that need to be done so we don't have to face the fear. Part of us wants to ride, wants to enjoy this time and wants to get closer to our dream. But part of us is scared of what might happen, what could happen and wants us to stay safe. The frustration we feel, the disappointment in ourselves, comes from the conflict between these parts.

What if we could get them working *together*?

After all, both parts want us to be happy, right? One wants us to ride and be happy, the other wants to be safe and we want to be both. What if, instead of letting our unconscious hold us hostage to our fear, what if we can get these two parts to *negotiate* a settlement they can both live with? What a great idea. Like all great ideas, it's one thing having the idea, it's quite another knowing how to put it into practice.

There is a technique that can help with this and that is what I am going to share with you in this chapter. Some parts of the technique might seem a little weird, but it's based on what actually works for real people in these situations, so use it, and it will work for you.

The first thing to realise is that all these voices and feelings are coming from inside you, therefore they are all, in some way, looking out for you and your survival. Every one of these voices and feelings has a positive intent for you. Since they all have a positive intent, once we work out what that is, it should be possible to get them all working *for* us rather than what they so often appear to be doing, which is working against us. The easiest way to explain this is to write it out as a series of steps. Read through them, go through the steps as written and you will feel the change. It can help to do this with a friend and to coach each other through the process. This looks like a long process, but although there are a lot of steps it only takes about fifteen minutes to do effectively in most cases. Let's use the example of the two parts where one wants us to ride and have fun and the other one does *not* want us to ride.

1. **Open up the lines of communication**
   Invite the part of you that wants to ride to come out and talk to you. This is the easy one so we will do this one first!

2. **Give this part an image, or a feeling and a name** (for example mine is a centaur and is called Fred). The more specific you can be here, the better, size, colour, shape, feel, smell. One of my friends has a yellow blob called Sunshine, so it can be anything that feels right to you.

3. **Ask this part, "What is your positive intent for me?"**, and listen to the answer that will just come into your mind. Then say, "Thank you—and what does that do for me?". Repeat the, "Thank you—and what does that do for me?", three, five or seven times to make sure you get to a deep answer rather than the first thing you think of. The more specific, detailed answers you have for what this part does for you, the stronger it will be in the negotiation. Very often this part wants you to be happy, successful and enjoying yourself.

4. **Work out *where* this part of you is when you are talking with it.** You can invite it to move to an easier place. For me, this part usually sits on my left shoulder, and when I want to talk to it, it moves down to the palm of my left hand.

5. **Say thank you to this part of you** and ask it to stay around while you talk to the other part of yourself. You need to talk to *both* sides

6. **Now ask the other part of you to come out.** This is 'the part of me that does not want me to ride'. Remember this part is in your unconscious so might be a bit wary of exposing itself. You may need to say something like, "I know you are trying to help me and I want to hear more from you so I can pay you the attention you deserve.", to encourage it to trust you and come out to talk.

7. **Give this part an image, or a feeling and a name.** Funnily enough for me this part is a bit like Brian Blessed (I know, isn't it strange how our brains work? That friend of mine has a dark blue cube she calls 'Blue'. Whatever feels right to you).

8. **Ask this part, "What is your positive intent for me?"**, and listen to the answer that will just come into your mind. If you don't hear anything just ask again. Now here's the important thing, whatever comes into your mind, accept it and say thank you. Even if it sounds

ridiculous to your conscious mind. If it helps, think of your unconscious as being like a three-year old child trying to do the right thing. All good intent but not necessarily able to explain things very well. Then say, "Thank you—and what does that do for me?". Repeat the, "Thank you—and what does that do for me?", three, five or seven times to make sure you get to a deep answer rather than the first thing you think of. Sometimes this gets a bit emotional as you realise that a part of yourself you thought was a problem is actually working very hard to keep you safe and sound and genuinely has your best interests at heart. Really listen to what it has to say—the more it believes you are taking it seriously (when previously you have tried so hard to shut it down and keep it quiet) and the more helpful it will be. Sometimes it gets quite talkative, so be patient. Very often, this part ultimately says it wants you to be happy too, just in a safe way.

9. **Work out *where* this part of you is when you are talking with it.** Again, you can invite it to move to an easier place. For me, this part usually sits on my right shoulder, and when I want to talk to it, it moves down to the palm of my right hand.

10. **Say thank you to this part of you** and ask it to stay around and join in the conversation

11. **Breathe and relax**: you are on your way to negotiating with your Confidence Kidnappers. Now both parts are talking with you. Now you have both parts of yourself out and really understand the positive intent they both have for you. For some people, just at this point they feel a huge sense of relief as instead of fighting inside themselves, they now feel they are coherent and heading in the same direction.

12. **Now the next step is to get the two parts to talk to *each other*.**

13. **First, ask the part of you that wants to ride,** what it would like to say to the part that wants to keep you safe. And let it talk. You may find words coming into your head — say them. Whatever they are, just say them. When you believe that part is finished, say thank you.

14. **Now ask the part of you that wants to keep you safe** what it would like to say to the part of you that wants to ride.

    At this stage, you will hear a lot of common ground between the two parts. They will already be talking to each other constructively rather than in conflict.

15. **Now ask the part of you that wants to keep you safe**, "What would the other part, the part of me that wants to ride, have to do for you to allow me to ride?". Take your time here. This is your unconscious telling you what it needs to let go of the fear and let you move forward. Listen carefully. This is where you will find out what you need to do to be confident and not afraid.

16. **Now ask the part of you that wants to ride** what it will *agree* to do to keep the part of you that wants to keep you safe, happy. You will notice that they are starting to work together now. In fact, sometimes at this stage the conversation takes on a life of its own and you don't need the script any more.

17. **Now you as a mediator can take what you have heard from both parts of you, and draw up a contract**. This will sound something like this, "So, if the part of me that wants to ride does a, b, and c, then the part of me that wants to keep me safe will let me spend time with the horses and do a, b and c . But, if I do anything that causes me to go above 5 in my Confidence Score, then the part of me that keeps me safe reserves the right to stop me and make me nervous so I don't do it.". This will be the working agreement you will stick to, so make sure both parts agree to it, and work until you actually

find agreement. Usually, the first contract will be quite limited as your unconscious needs to learn to trust you. I suggest you agree to a limited amount of things (e.g. you can groom and do groundwork but not ride) but limit the time frame as well so agree to this for, say, one or two weeks and then do this exercise again.

18. **Before you finish the conversation,** make sure we finish on a good note: ask each part to give the other part a gift. You don't have to know what it is consciously, just put your hands together so the two parts can exchange their gifts.

19. **Now stick to the contract!**
    The hardest part is that now you have to go out there and stick to the agreement. You are not allowed to change it unless you renegotiate it with both parts of yourself.

After doing this, you feel more relaxed, more coherent and able to do things you previously avoided.

How does this process work? By bringing your unconscious mind into a conscious conversation, you increase your awareness of yourself and your true feelings, remove denial and stay safe. By building trust you build confidence. Remember that the origin of the word confidence is the Latin 'with trust'.

I used this process with Martin who had come to me concerned about his internal conflict. As he described it, part of him really wanted to climb the career ladder at work and get to the top ranks of leadership. At times this was the most important thing to him in his life. However, every time an opportunity came up to make progress another part of him said it wasn't worth doing. Martin worked through this process and discovered that the negative voice (which in his mind was Patrick Stewart the actor) had the positive intent of making sure he kept his work life balance healthy and didn't jeopardise his relationships with his wife and children. Something his own father had *not* been successful with.

The part of him that wanted to climb the career ladder (which was the actor Jim Carrey) was driving for not just financial security but for proving he had made the 'right' decision leaving the family business and striking out in a completely different field of business.

Martin worked through the steps and although at first he found it difficult to come up with a contract that would work for both voices, together we were able to finally create one that both his parts felt content with. A large part of his contract was putting in place ways to track his work life balance so he could get 'early warning' of any issues, and planning actions to pre-empt those issues.

After this process, Martin found that his internal conflict was resolved and, as he stuck to the contract and proved he was working *with* his concerns rather than against them, he found his confidence returning and was able to focus on achieving his goals in a way that worked for him and his family.

It is important to have a time limit in your contract, because this is what allows you to later change the contract as things progress. Give yourself an initial two week time limit, then have this conversation with the parts again and you will usually find that things have moved forward significantly and you can agree a completely new contract. Often after a couple of 'rounds' your unconscious will have built sufficient trust in you and how your conscious mind is taking care of yourself that it will leave the conversation completely and you will have resolved the conflict.

So when you hear those 'Confidence Kidnappers' whispering to you, you can now have a conversation with them and get them working *with* you instead of against you and this will definitely expand your Confidence Zone!

## Just one more thing

### Remember the bigger picture

If at any stage during this process your unconfidence or fear increases—stop and change the conversation. This happened in a recent meeting with a client when she realised as we were asking her two parts to work together that she found this idea increased her feelings of fear. To give some context, the two parts were her right to challenge people, and her need not to upset people. When we paused the process and asked each of the parts in turn *why* her fear increased when she thought of them agreeing on an approach, we uncovered that when they had done this before (which was news to her!) they had been protecting her. When she asked what they were protecting her from, she remembered an incident from her college days where she had been in a very challenging situation and had needed to resort to physical violence to get herself to safety. In that situation her right to challenge and her need not to upset people had declared a truce and this violent person had emerged. Now, that had kept her safe in that dangerous situation but it had also scared her—not so much the situation, but the realisation that she had that capacity for physical violence inside her. Since then, she had blocked that memory and that part of her identity.

When you do this process and notice fear or unconfidence *increasing* it usually means that there is another part that needs to be involved in the process, often a part that has been hidden up to now. My recommendation is if this happens to you, then find a good coach and get some support through the process, as dealing with three or four Confidence Kidnappers is a bit more challenging than just two!

For most people, with two clear parts causing conflict and unconfidence, then negotiating with the parts is a great way to expand the Confidence Zone!

# CHAPTER 9
## HOW TO USE YOUR FEAR TO EXPAND YOUR CONFIDENCE ZONE

*"Fear keeps us focused on the past or worried about the future. If we can acknowledge our fear, we can realise that right now we are okay. Right now, today, we are still alive, and our bodies are working marvellously. Our eyes can still see the beautiful sky. Our ears can still hear the voices of our loved ones."* —Thich Nhat Hanh, Buddhist monk and peace activist

Fear is a powerful thing.

Fear of being hurt, fear of losing control, fear of not knowing what to do, fear of what might happen, fear of looking stupid, fear of damaging others, fear of hurting ourselves, fear of failing, fear of what if we succeed? Fear of not being good enough, fear of being too good. Fear of change, fear of not changing, fear of not being able to change...

We give power to this fear by fighting it, denying it. In denying the fear, trying to pretend it's not really there, we ignore the whispers of self-doubt. But the self-doubt doesn't go away. It's there for a reason, and so when we don't hear it, it has to raise its voice and shout louder and louder to get our attention—and so that slight anxiety we push ourselves through and ignore, grows into nausea, legs shaking and tears when we even think of doing things.

In fighting the fear, we give it power. The fear is from within ourselves, so it is like fighting a reflection. Every ounce of energy we put into fighting the fear feeds into the energy the fear itself has to use against us. We fight ourselves and tear ourselves apart. The fear grows louder, stronger until there is room for nothing else. Opposition breeds opposition. Resistance builds resistance. Aggression and anger towards our fear is aggression and anger towards ourselves. We become violent to ourselves when we deny the fear, or fight it and try to force it away. We are forcing ourselves against ourselves. Can you imagine the damage this does?

It is not fear that is harmful to us. Fear is just our unconscious trying to keep us safe. It is the fear of fear that causes the harm. By being frightened of the fear, and denying or fighting it, we give it a strange power over us—a power of control, of limitation and we allow the fear to stop us from living. And we are fighting a part of ourselves. A part that is just trying to keep us safe.

When we fight ourselves, we are not coherent or congruent and everyone around us knows this. The violence and conflict inside us transmits to our family, our friends, our horses. How do you think that impacts them?

In my coaching work, with people in business and with the equestrians I coach, I see a lot of people with fear. I see tense riders, forceful riders. I see riders whose hands are tight on the reins, who cannot breathe while on their horse and I see horses tense and armoured against the abrupt, grasping movements of their frightened rider. I see people at work. People whose whole demeanour and attitude changes as they cross that threshold into their office, as if they are 'girding their loins' for another tough day at the office. I see the people around them reacting to this by putting on their own armour and being ready to argue.

I see very few people riding without fear. I see very few calm, relaxed people who step onto their horse as they would onto a friend, and who can sit with a loose rein and rub their horse as they greet their partner. I see very few people walking into their workplace as relaxed and confident as they walk into their own house, or who walk into a meeting with the same confidence that they would meet a group of friends they are playing sport with. I see a lot of people who are holding fear in their hearts, and it is getting in the way of them enjoying their life. It is getting in the way at work, at home and in the rest of life.

It is the same fear.

Fear is the enemy of art and creativity. It produces tense, tight people who make tense tight movements and who not only change their own behaviour, but change the behaviour of the people around them. Frightened people end up reacting instead of responding, shouting instead of listening and fighting instead of focusing.

Fear leads to 'armouring' where we wrap ourselves tight against possible harm, where we build a barrier between ourselves and others, or ourselves and the external world, so it can't hurt us. Except just building that barrier hurts us. It cuts us off from everything we need to enjoy life including friends, family, empathy and connection.

Fear causes us to brace instead of relax. This stresses us, and also is noticed by others—they feel that tension and brace in us and so they brace in return. Suddenly everyone is tense and braced, communication is not working as it used to and we feel out of control and that just increases the fear.

Fear makes our muscles tight and even when we try to move softly and lightly, the tightness from the fear means our movements are bigger, jerkier and cruder than we imagine, our voices are louder and harsher than we intend.

The biggest thing about fear? With fear, we cannot feel. Without feeling we cannot connect and that means there can't be any harmony around us. So often we take that feeling of harmony for granted, that things will run smoothly, that we can predict how people will react to things and how things will happen. When fear kicks in it's as if all that falls apart, the harmony disappears and everything is out of tune.

Now think about what fear does to you. What does it do to you at work and in your life? What do you hold on to tightly, when do you tense up? What do you armour against? When do you find yourself reacting out of fear instead of responding with confidence?

So—we need to let go of fear. Easier said than done! What happens when someone tells you to, "Let go of fear."? Most of us hold on even tighter.

First, we need to recognise that fear is our unconscious letting us know it doesn't think we are safe, so fear is most often our natural intelligence telling us something and to just simply remove the fear without any thought for the consequences would be dangerous. What else can we do? Many people talk of, "Fight the fear.", but we are going to talk about something different. Fear is a natural part of you, telling you to take care. Fear, just like the limiting beliefs we explored in Chapter 6, has a positive intent. So rather than think of fighting the fear, or ignoring it, or overcoming it—let's talk of *accepting* the fear. Accepting the fear to the extent we can work with it and work with our reality, rather than stay in our armoured world where it is impossible to do well or enjoy life.

How can we do that? There are a lot of things involved in fear—knowledge, understanding, trusting ourselves, investing in ourselves, self-awareness—many things.

The main thing we need to do before we can resolve fear is understand it—and ourselves. For most of us, fear is such a natural, normal integral part of who we are that it is actually very difficult to let go of it. To some extent it defines us and if we give it up what do we have left? Realising we actually have fear and letting it go is like losing a part of ourselves.

For some of us our image of ourselves has no fear, so to accept that we are actually frightened is too much for us, so we don't go there. Then something happens to bring it in to focus—a fall from a horse, a moment of fear in a meeting when we realised we had no idea what to say, a moment when we realise how close we were to not being safe—even just our age changes things.

What I have seen is that when we realise we are frightened, we go through the six stages of letting go, just as happens in so many important areas of our lives. Let me go through these stages, and you think about which ones you recognise, in yourself or friends, and how recognising this can help you in your plans for moving forward.

## Shock

For many of us it is an absolute shock when we realise we are frightened. When we recognise that feeling inside us as fear, we are often confused, frustrated and even disoriented. Often we have to go away from the source of the fear, and hide out somewhere safe and secure as we feel so disturbed by this realisation. This shock can be quite a deep one and threaten our very identity so this can be a very uncomfortable and scary time.

## Denial

The next stage is to pretend it isn't happening. I come across a lot of people who are in this stage. People who say: "I had a fall, I had a fright—but I'm fine now."; "Yes, my legs wobble and I cry a bit—but I'm fine really."; "I always have butterflies but my boss tells me to get over it and once I am on that stage I am ok."; "This isn't happening to me, I'm not afraid!". Sometimes I can see they are telling the truth, but other times the tightness and tension in their body gives them away—they are most certainly *not* fine.

The risk of getting stuck in this stage is that everyone else most definitely knows you are *not* ok and this is often where the spirals begin. Your nerves feed other people's nerves which feed your nerves until you are in a very bad place. Often this bad place is what finally spins you out of denial, but it's not a pleasant journey.

How else can we get out of denial? Well you often can't do this by yourself. For most of us it's other people who help us out by saying something to make us realise we have an issue we can resolve. Most of the people I work with come to me because other people have made it clear to them that something is wrong and it is having an impact.

## Anger

The first step out of denial usually involves anger—anger at yourself for being so weak and ineffective, for being out of control of your feelings and not being able to sort this out yourself. Your inability to stop feeling frightened irritates, annoys and finally angers you. Some people stop at this stage—and stay angry at themselves, using that anger for motivation to keep going. In this stage I see people with gritted teeth, short sharp breathing and staccato movements and voices. The anger comes out in big clumsy movements of the body and voice, and this is where aggression often comes out. Sometimes the anger internalises, and you become endlessly self-critical. Almost always, other people around you respond to this stage by becoming defensive, putting effort into avoiding you—which has its own impact on you. As other people armour themselves against the impact of your fear, you find yourself increasingly isolated and 'unfairly judged'.

There is one good thing about the anger—it can make you sit up and notice there is a real issue here, which can lead to action.

## Bargaining

The most common action we take is bargaining. "I'll just do some deep breathing and I will be fine". I will share a horse related example here to show how subtle this phase can be and the impact it can have. The horse-people I coach are often in this stage of fear: they have had the shock of realising they are frightened, and worked through the anger and now the conversation in their head goes something like this:

"I'll just go ride for ten minutes, then nothing bad will happen.".

We bargain with ourselves. We also bargain with the horse.

"I won't ask you to do canter, if you stay safe and reliable at trot.".

Most of our horse bargaining happens at a subconscious level, but when I talk to people about this stage they often laugh and share the bargains they now realise they were making in their horsemanship and riding. "If I never ask you anything you don't want to do, you will keep me safe.", is an implicit bargain a lot of us have in this stage. The great thing about this stage is that we feel back in control again. By making the bargain, we feel we have managed our fear, and it will let us get on with our lives. In fact what we have done is created for ourselves a tiny Comfort Zone where we will stay stuck forever creating new bargains unless something else happens.

Now that was a horse example—what parallels can you see in areas of your life? For example, this is a common place where people get stuck in relationships. Luckily though, this stage almost inevitably leads to the next one as the bargains we make end up being broken. Our horse does buck in trot, our horse does nap even when we take a safe route, our partner doesn't stop drinking, our boss doesn't stop picking on us—and so on. When this happens, the next stage is depression.

## Depression

Depression usually comes out of a failure to meet your own expectations e.g. when bargains are not fulfilled. When the horse lets us down by returning to the behaviour that scared us (not surprising really since the horse had no idea he had signed up to the bargain in the first place!), then our expectations have not been met and we feel let down, sometimes even betrayed by our horse and our horsemanship. Sometimes, when our horse *does* accidentally live up to their side of the bargain we realise that this hasn't really fixed anything, we are still scared and now we are 'stuck' with the bargain and can't move on. That leads to depression too.

It's the same with people and relationships. A partner lets us down by returning to the behaviour we thought we had bargained would not happen. A common one there is, "If I keep things light and no pressure then they will not lose their temper with me.". Then they do lose their temper and we realise our bargain didn't work—and we move onto this stage, depression.

A challenge with depression is that it is a mental state that is associated with *inaction* so it is quite hard to get out of by yourself. This is where having friends and other people who can support you is key to moving on to the next stage. Otherwise you may end up staying in the pit of despair (see the Kisses and Kittens confidence trap in the next section). When we are depressed we don't feel like doing anything. Our mind asks, "What is the point? Why bother? Maybe I should give up—find my horse another home, get another job, walk away before it all goes completely wrong.".

And yet it *is* just a stage in the process, and if we have the support network to get through this stage, then the chances are we can move on to the last stage.

## Acceptance

Nothing really changes. We still have the fear, we still are scared of things we want to do, and yet everything has changed because now we *accept* we are afraid. We accept we are unconfident, worried and that the fear is real and affecting us. Now we accept it, we can decide to do something about it. This is the stage when people look around and ask for help. Help from from friends, colleagues, yard owners, confidence coaches, and are ready to move on. Only once you are at this stage can you accurately analyse your fear and decide whether it is rational (it is keeping you safe) or irrational (you are safe but need to persuade your unconscious to believe you) and make a plan to move forwards by starting your Confidence Journey.

## Why does this matter?

For yourself, knowing these stages are a natural part of the process will allow you to relax and go through them. Maybe you will recognise where you are in the journey and yes, a good coach can help move you along a bit faster. There is no fixed timeline on this path. Some people move through all the stages in a single conversation, others take longer. It depends on many things. However, knowing the stages in the journey can stop you from panicking when you find yourself feeling angry or depressed and you can say, "Ah, I'm at *that* stage now.". By not fighting the process, but understanding it you can manage it better and give yourself permission to experience it in order to get to acceptance as soon as possible and start moving forwards. You will also know when you are 'stuck' which increases the chances of being able to ask for help.

Another way this matters is when you are helping other people. These stages are necessary. If we skip a stage, we end up looping back to it so if you notice a friend who is frightened or unconfident and you understand this process, instead of chivvying them along, or telling them to get help, work out where they are and be with them in that stage. Connect with them in that moment, and help them where they actually are. If you can do that, then their journey will be shorter and sweeter and they will be able to move on much sooner than if they are rushed along, or if your support doesn't match where they are in the process.

If you have ever wondered why someone doesn't follow your very sensible advice take a look and see where they are in this process—that might explain it! For ourselves and our friends, giving permission to be where we are in coming to terms with our fear is important to us not getting stuck and reaching the acceptance stage where, finally, we can ask for, and hear, the help and support that is all around us.

So now we understand a bit more about fear, and the stages we go through—what can we *do* about it? Well first of all let me ask you how do you treat someone *else* who is frightened?

Would we shout at her? Tell her not to be so stupid? Not to be frightened? Would we deny it? Tell her she's not frightened, or shouldn't be? Tell her to ignore her fear? We wouldn't do that to a friend and yet so many of us do it to ourselves.

What if instead of denying or fighting fear, we welcome it? That, after all is true acceptance. What if we said, "Thank you.", to it for keeping us safe, and stopping us from doing dangerous things? "Thank you.", for causing me to think about what I do, so I take care of myself. After all, I deserve to take care of myself. I am worth it.

What if we said that? What if we were *thankful* for our fear? What if we made the fear feel welcome, comfortable, relaxed and trusting. Well then we could have a conversation with it, just like we would have a conversation with a friend.

"Hi there, thanks for keeping me safe, I realise you are doing an important job. I would like to respect the job you do. I would also like to be happy riding my horse/going to work/leading meetings. How can I set things up so that both things can be true?".

You may be surprised to hear your fear answer you, give you some ideas. Usually, it will suggest taking smaller steps, breaking things down into tinier increments, making sure you are safe at one step before going on to the next.

When Chris felt fear about getting back into dating after a bad breakup, he recognised that he actually had not just a lack of confidence but fear. The fear was stopping him from even talking to women he didn't already know which limited his options for the future significantly. In our coaching session he asked himself, "What has to happen so I can respect my fear, stay safe—and date again?".

He listened and instead of just going back on the internet dating sites and starting to meet people—he broke it down into smaller steps. He joined a couple of social groups in his area that did the same hobbies as him—a walking group and an art group. He went on several activity-focused get-togethers a few times until he was able to speak comfortably with male and female group members with confidence and ease. When he realised he had no fear about just talking to women he didn't know in an activity environment, he then joined his friends on more purely social evenings out where he practised speaking to women he didn't know. He wasn't trying to 'date' these women, he was practising talking with his fear and it was allowing him to make progress. He set a rule of not actually dating for three months but focusing on the steps he could take to work with his fear.

As he went through this process he realised something interesting— the quality of his interactions with women changed significantly. He became more interested in them as people rather than as his 'potential date', which changed his whole demeanour and theirs. He discovered that he was able to be his genuine self with women he met and they still found him interesting. He realised that for a lot of his life he had been playing a role when he dated, trying to project the perfect partner rather than his authentic self—which inevitably led to challenges in the relationship later on when he let the real self leak through and his partner felt he was changing and not the person they had 'signed up for'.

When we start working *with* our fear we often get surprising answers. Chris learned a lot about himself on his fear-friendship programme.

So did Amanda when she reached the stage of accepting her fear after a fall from her horse. She had not been hurt too badly, but had been surprised to experience the shock, denial, anger and depression aspects of her fear. It was when one of her friends pointed out to her how she was constantly bargaining with her horse and how ridiculous this was (after all the horse had no idea of the bargains!) that she fully accepted that she was actually frightened of riding. After trying many different approaches to working through her fear, she asked to work with me and was surprised when the first thing I asked her to do was thank her fear for keeping her safe. As she did this, I could see her shoulders lower, her neck relax and her whole posture soften. She felt the difference too, "I feel as if this is going to work.".

To prove to her fear that she was taking safety seriously, we broke down riding her horse again into small, incremental steps where she would constantly check in with her fear so it didn't have to shout at her. She went through many steps including saddling her horse up and unsaddling him, standing on the mounting block next to him and getting down again, putting a foot in the stirrup and out again, putting weight in the stirrup and out again, standing fully in the stirrup and down again and then swinging a leg over and back again… and each time the exercise was repeated ten times.

Ten times? Yes, because the first few times the fear was high. Above 5 on the scale. As she did the exercise more times, her unconscious realised that she was serious about working *with* her fear and the number came down into her Confidence Zone. By the end of an hour she was on her horse, walking around the arena, with a score of 1-2. All the way through she had accepted that her fear was working to keep her safe, and it was allowing her to make progress. It was also talking to her in a whisper, not a shout.

Amanda's insight when she went through this process was that often in the past she had done a lot of these steps on autopilot, not fully paying attention. She realised that on the day of her fall there had been several indications that her horse was not happy being ridden, which she had missed or ignored in her rush to get on with things. Interestingly, she realised that this was a pattern in other areas of her life. Making friends with her fear had positive consequences in many areas for her.

By taking these small steps, both these people proved to their fear that they *were* safe, that they could handle things. The end result was that their fear became their partner and worked with them on keeping them safe while they still achieved their goals and were happy.

## Just one more thing

### Fear is important, it matters

Fear shrinks our Confidence Zone. If we don't deal with our fear, our lives get smaller and smaller. This is why working with fear is so important, it is a life stealer. It overpowers our dreams. Welcoming your fear, being thankful for your fear – takes the power away from the fear. It makes the fear our partner. It means we are working with ourselves, not against ourselves.

Working with our fear instead of against it gives the power back to where it belongs...

...with ourselves

# CHAPTER 10
## WEIRD AND WONDERFUL WAYS OTHER PEOPLE HAVE EXPANDED THEIR CONFIDENCE ZONES

*"There are a thousand ways to kneel and kiss the ground; there are a thousand ways to go home again."*— Rumi, Sufi mystic

In the previous chapters in this section I have shared the five most powerful ways to expand your Confidence Zone. In the next section, Part 3, we will explore the five biggest traps with confidence building and also look at five tips that will accelerate your Confidence Journey.

Before we leave this section though, I wanted to share with some of the other ways people have succeeded in expanding their Confidence Zones, so you can see what else works and what resonates with you. To do this I will share five stories.

## Story 1: A sense of humour

Remember Sarah and Sioned from Part 1? Two experienced managers who were so terrified of having to present at a national conference that they almost turned the opportunity down? Luckily they had a very supportive area manager who invited me to work with them. For Sarah, realising that it was a lack of knowledge in how to create an interesting presentation, and a lack of practice at the skills required meant she was able to solve her anxiety by investing time and effort in coaching on both these things. By the time the conference came around she had done her presentation several times onto video for feedback and with her branch team as a test audience. She knew it was good, and that *she* was good, which boosted her confidence.

For Sioned, it was more complicated. Although she identified the same knowledge and skills issues as Sarah, she also realised that she found it extremely difficult just being up on a stage in front of an audience. Regardless of how confident she was in her content, and how much she was able to show great delivery skills in practice, she was still concerned that performance anxiety would be her issue. We put on a test presentation with the area Leadership Team and she struggled to demonstrate the skills we knew she had. Sioned realised she felt as if she was not offering real value to her audience and would be letting them down with her talk. So we came up with a creative idea—we employed a cartoonist to work with her on her slides.

For each piece of her talk, instead of the usual slides, we had an original cartoon that made people laugh out loud as it came up on the screen. That laughter had the effect of relaxing Sioned, making her feel the audience was on her side and she was giving them something entertaining and interesting. She aced her presentation. Interestingly after that she never had the stage fright effect again, so that one process had expanded her Confidence Zone.

Taking something that seems stressful and turning it into humour works for a lot of people—as in the next story.

## Story 2: Rewriting the script

Pietro had a bad experience a year ago. At the time he had known his English wasn't fluent enough for him to be confident leading the project team at the conference, which is what his boss had asked him to do. Initially he had said no and explained why, but had then allowed himself to be pressured into it. The conference had been the disaster he had predicted. For him it had been one stressful moment after another, and the feedback from the participants had been negative. He felt his career had been set back by the whole experience.

Since then Pietro had been working hard. He had transformed his language capability and developed his team leadership skills significantly. However, he still seemed stuck in the negative experience from the past. Every time a conference was mentioned, Pietro would go into his story of how awful his last experience had been.

Pietro came to me after friends and family encouraged him to try to move on, especially as there was another big conference coming up where they wanted him to succeed. He had tried many approaches, but none had really worked and the negative emotions and feelings from the event were still overwhelming.

We applied a technique focused on changing how he saw his memory. We took his memory, and played with every sub-modality in it. Sub-modalities are the elements making up a memory and include whether you are in the memory or standing on the outside observing it, the colours you see, the feelings you have, the sounds you hear—everything to do with your senses and how they engage with the memory. When Pietro described his memory he was fully 'in the memory', he could clearly recall colours and sounds and the words he used made it clear that this was a tragedy in tone. So, for his case, we re-ran it as an old silent movie comedy in black and white, with him watching it from the cheap seats, laughing at every ridiculous moment where he had made poor decisions. After he had run his memory this way a few times, he was genuinely laughing at the situation he had got himself into and had successfully changed the memory, and the way he described it, from tragedy to comedy.

This is a tried and tested NLP (neuro-linguistic programming) technique and accessing the resources of an NLP coach can be great way of expanding your Confidence Zone.

## Story 3: Mindfulness and meditation

Remember Caroline? The artist who had stopped drawing because of the limiting beliefs from her childhood? For her, expanding her Confidence Zone came from learning mindfulness and meditation. Her biggest struggle was with the negative voices she had in her head telling her that there was no point doing her art, even though once she started a piece she felt great happiness and joy. She had worked with the Confidence Kidnappers exercise, but it seemed she had to keep repeating it to be able to keep drawing.

So we took a different approach. Mindfulness has been proven to reduce anxiety and enhance perspective-setting, so she completed an eight-week mindfulness course. On this course, and with her subsequent meditation practice, she found that when she practised regularly, her reaction to the negative voices changed completely. She was able to see them as simply voices from her past which were no longer relevant. When they spoke up saying, "You are not the best, you never will be, why bother?", she started responding with a shrug and a, "So what, I enjoy it, that's enough.", attitude which made a huge difference.

Within twelve months she was exhibiting her stunning drawings at a local gallery and was happy to be enjoying her art again.

Mindfulness and meditation are great tools for putting limiting beliefs and voices from your childhood into perspective, and enabling your unconscious mind to let go of things that might have been useful in the past but are no longer relevant now.

## Story 4: A different perspective

Diane had been experiencing a lot of anxiety at work. She was anxious about her performance, her capability and also about whether she was as career focused as she felt she 'should be'. Sources of stress were her concerns as to whether she looked the part, was dressed right, acted right—there were a lot of issues impacting her. Conversation showed these came from many sources and we started unravelling some of them in our sessions. Part way through the process, Diane volunteered to join a group going to Tanzania to build schools for local children. She was away for six weeks and when she returned, she was almost a different person. All the anxieties appeared to have resolved. When we talked, Diane shared that seeing how people lived there, how little they had and how they coped and still found happiness had put her own anxieties into perspective. She reprioritised her life, downsized her work to spend more time with her young children and experienced much greater happiness. For her, this trip expanded her Confidence Zone and made a huge difference to her happiness and enjoyment of her life.

Sometimes we get so caught up in our own worlds we forget that we are not the centre of the universe, and a way to reset our perspective can be invaluable.

One last story, with a warning of what can happen if you aren't paying attention.

## Story 5: Routines, rituals and superstition

It's quite common for us to use routines as a way to build and sustain our confidence. Before important meetings we might have certain clothing we prefer to wear, certain patterns of behaviour such as having a particular breakfast or coffee beforehand. In the horse riding world we have many routines. Some are practical in terms of grooming and safely saddling up but some are habits we develop to make ourselves feel better. However, the trouble with routines is that they can become rituals and superstitions and then instead of helping our confidence, they can actually damage it.

Claude seemed to have successfully overcome his fear of presenting. He had gone from shaking with nerves to being able to consistently achieve top ranking for his sessions at his company's national conferences. Then, one day, it all fell apart. Colleagues saw him nervous and shaky before going on stage, his performance was clumsy and clunky and he had none of his usual fluency and impact. What had happened?

What had started for Claude as a routine of being smartly dressed and calmly practising some breathing exercises, had turned into a ritual which he had performed identically before every presentation. In this ritual it was the same shirt, the same suit, the same breathing exercises done in exactly the same order. However, somewhere in that process of going from a routine which allowed some flexibility, to a ritual that has strict elements and order, superstition had crept in.

A routine is a set of behaviours we prefer to perform. A ritual is when that preference becomes a fixed pattern. Superstition is when beliefs form, which underlie that ritual. When superstition comes into play, the impact of *not* doing the ritual or not completing it in some way is almost always negative. When behaviour falls into belief, it is passing from the conscious to the unconscious mind, and we have had many discussions on the implications of that. A superstition underlying a ritual basically makes that ritual a contract with the unconscious: if I do this ritual, then I will be ok on stage. Therefore if we *don't* do the ritual, what does the unconscious do? Claude had found out. After that, he took care to make sure that his pre-presentation routines stayed flexible and conscious and did not fall into ritual and superstition.

This is definitely something to think about as you work on expanding your Confidence Zone. Sometimes a behaviour that seems helpful in the short term can lead to longer term issues so be careful!

## Just one more thing

## How many ways can you expand your Confidence Zone?

These are the ways I find most useful in my Confidence Coaching work. There are more stories and examples of how people have expanded their Confidence Zone on the website. Remember, the best way is to use the Confidence Journey every time you have a concern—not only will you expand your own Confidence Zone but you will become more practiced at the Journey and be able to effectively coach yourself in any situation.

Now we have looked at some ways people have successfully expanded their Confidence Zones, let's move on to Part 3 where we explore the five biggest Confidence Traps people fall into, and share the five tips which will accelerate your Confidence Journey.

# PART 3
## CONFIDENCE TRAPS AND TIPS: FIVE TRAPS TO AVOID AND FIVE TIPS TO ACCELERATE YOUR CONFIDENCE JOURNEY

In my experience there are five common Confidence Traps that people fall into that can jeopardise their Confidence Journey. Here they are, along with some ideas for how to deal with them. They are followed by five great tips for accelerating your Confidence Journey. Knowing both the traps and the tips will make a real difference to your success.

# CONFIDENCE TRAPS TO AVOID

## Trap 1
### Pushing through: Why 'just doing it' doesn't always work — and when it sometimes does!

One thing a lot of us hear when we are not confident, is, "Just get on with it.". How often do we hear this? How often do people say, "Just give them a push and they will be fine!". Or, "Just get on and do it, you will be great once you get going."? Does it work? Should we give people a push or not? Let's look at a different perspective on this one. When someone asks an, "Is X better than Y?" type question, we can change that question to, "*When* is X appropriate, and *when* is Y appropriate?". If we do that we can then ask ourselves *when* is it appropriate to give someone that push and *when* is that the worst possible thing we can do?

Here's an example I often use in my workshops. Let's think about someone standing on the edge of a pool, hesitating about whether to jump in. When *might* it be ok to give them a little nudge, some 'help' to get in the water? *If* the person has been in before, knows how to swim, says they will be fine once they get in there, and just needs help getting in, then they might even be grateful when we encourage them with a little gentle push. Once in, they will swim away happily and there will be no hard feelings. But what if the person *doesn't* know how to swim and *won't* be fine once they are in? Giving *this* person a gentle shove will push them into a terrifying situation where their life will be at risk—and they will never trust you again and will be even more scared of standing near the edge of a pool in future.

I shared this story in one workshop and a woman in the audience suddenly realised why she had never liked standing near her father around water: he had given her that nudge and it had terrified her.

I agree there is a place for the 'grit your teeth and do it' approach. If you have ever had a really important presentation and you just have to do it, no matter how you feel then you will just get on with it. However, we need to make sure that if we push ourselves through what is a Confidence Threshold, putting us outside our Confidence Zone, that we aren't making it worse for the *next* time.

You may notice this with other people. You can ask them to do a presentation and they grit their teeth and do it, once and maybe twice. Then the third time you ask them they just can't grit their teeth anymore and they get sick, or refuse and you wonder why. This doesn't just happen with people. It happens with horses too. If our horse is worried about something they will often grit their teeth and do it because they want to do what we are asking. They might even do it twice. But on the third time they will tell us how they really feel and we are surprised because we missed their lack of confidence the first couple of times and are mystified at the 'sudden change' in them. I have already said that fear and unconfidence are our unconscious mind's way of keeping us safe. If we don't listen to it when it tries to talk to us, it just turns up the volume and shouts.

One person I worked with had been doing this to herself: gritting her teeth every time she made a presentation, because she knew she 'ought' to be doing it, and everyone said it would get better.

It didn't, it got worse. She started feeling nauseous before each event. Then the nausea started while preparing, then when even thinking of starting to work on a presentation. It ended up with her feeling sick just seeing the PowerPoint programme on her computer screen. Just so you know, that person ended up as a frequent keynote speaker, so things *did* change. Things *can* change and it's so much easier when we understand what is happening, as then we can work out how to fix it.

The key is to be aware of how you feel about doing something, and know the difference between when 'just do it' is a good idea and when it is, in fact, the worst thing you can do.

## Trap 2
## Missing the bigger picture: The rest of your life matters too

Several times I have met people who see no reason for their lack of confidence, to *not* be confident. These are often people who have tried many approaches to improving their confidence that have not worked. They have had coaching, been to courses and workshops, and yet nothing seems to be changing. In these particular cases, the phrases they use are, "I feel as if something is getting in the way of my becoming confident.". This is an interesting situation. This can also happen when I am coaching someone: every time we find an answer to the confidence issue they seem blocked and can't move forward again.

I remember one person, Diane, who had a confidence issue around painting which had recently come up. I had arranged to meet her in her art studio for an initial session. Just before I was due to leave to drive to her, a journey of over an hour and a half, she called and said she would rather come and see me. Since this was obviously important to her, I agreed and in a couple of hours we were sitting outside in the sunshine, looking over a lovely view as we talked.

We did the usual thing and started by working through the five steps of her Confidence Journey. But there seemed to be something blocking her. Every time we reached a point where she started relaxing and saying, "Yes, that could work…" it was as if a barrier came up inside her which said, "No, that can't happen.". So after about 45 minutes, I paused and said, "I just have one question for you: picture yourself 18 months from now, you're doing your art in your studio happily, there are finished paintings all around you and you're looking forward to your exhibition at the local gallery. It's all feeling absolutely wonderful, with no tension or worry. What else is happening?".

She looked down and said, "My husband has left me.".

Well, I certainly wasn't expecting *that*.

However, what wasn't unusual was that she was saying something *else* in her life was getting in the way of her becoming confident and this can happen more often than you might think.

We talked about this. I should probably make clear that she has given her permission for me to share her story here as it makes such a good learning point that confidence with one area of our life isn't always an isolated issue, it can be a reflection of larger concerns in our lives. In this case, it turned out there were some things going on in their relationship that led her to believe that if she was happy and confident, then her husband would leave her. Digging deeper, they had moved a few years ago to follow a dream of creating a home for their children and had worked hard for several years to rebuild a house and outbuildings so that holiday visitors would bring in the income they needed. This project was almost finished, was working well, and once that was done, Diane had concerns over what would keep her husband with her and the family. She mentioned that he always had to be busy doing something, and she worried that the relaxing life she wanted would not be exciting enough for him. We switched the coaching session to this topic and Diane had some plans when she went home.

She later contacted me to say that they had talked, her husband was starting another project (river trips and microlight flights for visitors!) and all was going well. Oh and by the way, her art was going well too. Apparently her confidence issues had slowly evaporated as the relationship issues had been resolved. Further conversation revealed that she had probably been picking up on her husband's feelings of, "What next after this project?", and he *had* been looking for what to move on to but just in terms of projects, not relationships!

This example raises the interesting concept of how our *ecology* can affect our ability to make changes. If you think of ecology as our whole environment, where we live, who we live with and all the expectations, habits and history too, it is easy to see that sometimes changes can be hard to make. Even changes that we want to make for ourselves and our happiness, might be hard to think about and do when we start thinking about the consequences these changes could have in the rest of our lives.

One person I worked with on confidence had to do some hard work, not on herself, but on her family so *they* could cope with the newly confident woman. They had become so used to her being 'the person who always said yes to helping others' that when she decided to focus on doing some things for herself, it was a big shock to everyone. This is an example of the external ecology being impacted by changes you may decide to make.

It is also important to check your *internal* ecology: will the change you are anticipating have any consequences other than the expected benefit? One ecology check I always run with clients is the following four questions where I ask them to put themselves three months from now and say:

Three months from now:

- I made this change — what has happened?
- I made this change — what hasn't happened?
- I didn't make this change — what has happened?
- I didn't make this change — what hasn't happened?

With these four questions, your unconscious will let you know how the change you are planning will fit into your internal ecology and identify any tweaks you need to make for it to be effective. However, remember also to ask that question I asked Diane:

"In 18 month's time, when all this is sorted, and I am confident, what *else* is happening?".

Listen to the first answer that comes into your mind. Whatever comes into your mind, however ridiculous or small or big or *anything*, is what needs to be sorted out before you will allow yourself to become confident. It's often useful to have a friend or coach with you when you do this, as this can lead to some challenging answers.

Remember though, in many of the cases I have worked with, the issues have been resolved happily. In an earlier post I mentioned that the unconscious mind is a bit like a three-year old child: it feels emotions but isn't always accurate with its analysis of things as per the story above. The unconscious is excellent at picking up feelings and undercurrents but will often label them with words and titles that are from our *own* baggage. Having a friend or coach to support you in that step can be very useful.

Forgetting to take *ecology* into account is a big Confidence Trap.

# Trap 3
## Kisses and kittens: The friends that keep you frightened

When we feel fear or lose confidence, or something happens that hurts us, we all want somewhere safe to hide out for a while. For many of us this is friends, family or sometimes a place on social media. We look for somewhere where we know others will understand our situation, will have felt the same way and will know exactly what we are going through. This is great. One very helpful thing we need to know when we lose confidence, or have a bad situation is that we are not alone. Having a safe, warm place where we can get hugs and comfort is very important when we are feeling low, fragile or incomplete. We need the wounds to our bodies, souls and psyches to heal a bit before we can move on.

If we are lucky, we find that place. Sometimes we are not so lucky and we end up in our own spiralling pit of misery. I know because I have been there. If you're reading this, chances are you have too, or know someone who has. That is a horrible experience feeling at the bottom of the pit, knowing the light is out there, but no idea of how to reach the light or even if you deserve the light. But if we are lucky we find a forum, a social networking page, a friend or some place we feel safe. Most of us want to lick our wounds then move on. But sometimes it is so warm and safe where we are, that it's difficult to think about moving outside that safety and going back out into the dangerous world again. I know many people who have found a safe place in routine, undemanding jobs when they are capable of, and actually want to do, so much more.

How do we leave our warm safe place? That is what this trap is about: the difference between safety and stagnation; comfort and closing down; how not to end up in a world of kisses and kittens that can seduce us into staying safe and scared forever.

I think we are all used to the idea that people *outside* our safe place might put time and effort into keeping us in there, not letting us out. There's the confident person who belittles our efforts to take it slow, the ones who run down our abilities making sure we stay where we feel incapable and unsure. Whenever we try to step outside our unconfident box, they push us firmly back in. How can we handle these people? Fundamentally one thing to ask yourself is, "What is their reason for doing this?". What is the benefit to them of you not being confident? Why does it matter so much to them that they are working *so* hard to stop you? Sometimes just asking that question unlocks your ability to go ahead regardless of them.

Now I am going to make a huge generalisation here but I will say that based on my own experience, when people make such a big fuss about something it's because they themselves have some issues around that something.

I was working with a small group of people who were building confidence in their skiing. We were on a lovely little ski slope that was perfect for this. It had a central slope that was smooth and easy, but also had a few bumps and moguls on one side, and some deep powder on the other, so you could stay safe when you wanted, and also play with the edges of your Confidence Zone when you wanted. The slope itself went in steps, so you could ski down about twenty metres then just head off to one side and rest there for a while. We were surrounded by trees, it was a clear sunny day and we were on this small, rather obscure well hidden slope well away from the main ski areas where things were a lot more challenging. It was the perfect safe place to practice playing with our Confidence Zones. As the group were building their confidence going from one side of the slope to the other, from one level area to the next, increasing their confidence in their ability to control their speed and direction, a mother and daughter appeared a short distance above us. They skied right into the middle of where we were practising and stopped, turned to face me and almost shouted:

"How long are you going to be in here? This is our favourite place to ski you know!".

I smiled and said, nice and calmly, "About ten or fifteen more minutes and we will feel safe enough to head across to that other area over there...", pointing to another slightly more challenging slope a few hundred meters away. Before I had even finished speaking, the mother said, with an angry tone:

"Well, this IS our favourite place and we need to be in here!".

I looked at her, she was tense and tight. Her face was braced, and her hands were tightly gripping her ski poles. Her daughter was also braced and tight and looked worried. What I saw was fear. I replied:

"OK. No problem, I know how good it is to be in a favourite place to ski. Let us just finish a couple of exercises and we will be out of your way and you can have the place to yourselves. It won't take long if you don't mind waiting.".

As I spoke I saw her shoulders lower and her hands soften a bit. We did our couple more exercises then headed off. What showed up as anger, aggression and almost bullying behaviour was, in my view, a reflection of the fear she felt while up there on that slope. I can guarantee that she does not think she has any confidence issues and that is what makes the fear turn into aggression.

There are many people outside their safe place who haven't acknowledged their own confidence concerns, wobbles and fears. These people will appear aggressive, angry and almost have a go at us for being unconfident, pushing and almost bullying us along. Once you realise that this is just a reflection of *their* issues, and really has nothing to do with you (other than the fact that you admitting your confidence issue and working on it confronts them with that possibility and threatens to make their fear real) it is so much easier to withstand them. Instead of getting upset with them look at their tension, their tightness and feel compassion for the fact they are so stuck inside their heads that they don't even *know* they have confidence issues.

However, there is something worse. It's something a lot of people are not aware of. Sometimes our supporters *inside* the pit can be as dangerous. Sometimes it's the other people in the safe place that won't let us leave. This is far more insidious and is often unconscious. After all, when we have found a safe warm place, and then we see someone beginning to leave us it is only natural to not want to see them go. This resistance can appear in direct form in comments such as, "Oh, I wouldn't do that.", "Are you sure that's safe?", "I wouldn't be doing that yet.", which raise questions in our conscious minds about whether we should be doing these things. Or it can be more indirect with comments like, "You are so brave to be doing that. I couldn't do it." which, while it sounds supportive, raises questions in our unconscious minds about whether we should be doing it or even thinking about it.

In both cases, the person or persons doing the resisting might have no idea what they are doing, or of the effect they are having. In fact they might truly believe they are being supportive and caring. After all, if you believe as I do that we all do the best we can with the resources we have available then I *do* believe that everyone in the pit is trying their best.

They are trying their best to be their best and do their best for everyone else. However, the *effect* of such behaviour can be to trap us in that pit, where we feel safe and secure, and stop us ever finding the confidence and resources to take those first steps out. We get so used to the kisses and kittens we forget about the soul enhancing joy that lies outside if only we could find a way to take those first steps.

When I thought about this particular Confidence Trap, two images came to mind. Both drawings start with a group of people sitting at the bottom of a pit on comfy sofas, hugging each other, and lots of kisses and kittens around them all. In the first picture, one person is leaving, going to the rainbow land above and every other person is working together to create a human ladder that can be used to safely and easily leave the pit. In the second, one person is trying to leave, and the others are hanging on to them and not allowing them to make the slightest move upwards towards the rainbow of growth.

Which pit are you in?

And do you know how to be the supporters in the first picture and not accidentally become the resistors in the second?

The aim of this book is to help you find your way out of the pit carrying all the love and warmth you found there with you on your journey.

## Trap 4

## Heroes and gurus: How The Guru Syndrome stops you getting true confidence

There is something out there that has an insidious effect on confidence. Whilst at the start it seems to make you confident, gives you the support you need to move forward, it actually erodes your self-belief and leaves you in a worse place than when you first started. Unfortunately this thing also appears to be a fundamental characteristic of human nature: it's something I call The Guru Syndrome.

This happens in all walks of life and has negative consequences wherever it occurs. It can happen intentionally or accidentally, but however it happens, ultimately it is a bad thing for you, your confidence, your knowledge and your life.

What is The Guru Syndrome? The Guru Syndrome is where you find someone who impresses you, inspires you, possibly educates you, and either they assume guru status—or you give it to them.

Let's look at the first. There are many coaches, trainers, leaders of programmes, and business owners out there who seem to be getting by quite nicely, then all of a sudden they change. Maybe they start believing their own publicity. They start believing their own myths and stories, they fall victim to their own magical thinking. One example that shows the start of The Guru Syndrome is when a person starts believing it is their special gift or talent that is making the difference, instead of realising that it is just what they are teaching and how they are teaching it that is achieving the results. When a teacher or coach changes from seeing themselves as a vehicle for communication, a bridge between a person and understanding, to seeing themselves as the *source* of that understanding, as the *only* source of that knowledge and understanding—that is when they can fall victim to The Guru Syndrome.

When, as a coach or teacher, you realise and accept that there is nothing particularly special about you, you just have a bit more knowledge or a few more resources than the people you are teaching, then you are pretty unlikely to develop The Guru Syndrome.

When I taught some massage techniques, which led to some huge changes and responses from people, it was very common for new learners to start thinking in a strange way: rather than thinking it was the *technique* being effective, they started talking about how their energy and 'special connection' was doing the work. They made the results they achieved the outcome of their special gift, their mystical energy, when it was their effective application of a learned technique that was really doing the work and getting the results. They were just the medium through which this technique could be applied. Now I am not saying for a moment that energy and connection isn't a key part of the process, in fact of *any* process. However, it's a fundamental truth that anyone who learned it could do it.

The Guru Syndrome can also happen intentionally. Someone can deliberately set out to establish themselves as a 'guru'. They plan and manipulate to get this status. However, this is rare. It is far more likely that this has happened accidentally. Maybe someone starts off as an instructor and gets a few good results. Maybe they get results where others have failed. Maybe they constantly hear how good they are so they start believing that they have something special. It's very tempting, it's very seductive. We all want to feel good about ourselves, and find something worthy in ourselves, something special. We all want self esteem. However, this is self esteem built on a false foundation which then of course leads to its own issues. If your confidence comes from something that is ultimately false, what will happen? You become defensive, you become rigid, you become inflexible.

So if you have coaches, trainers or mentors who fit that description, the likelihood is that they have fallen victim to their own version of The Guru Syndrome. And I say 'fallen victim' because they are victims. Once you are stuck in The Guru Syndrome, you are trapped against hearing anything else, seeing anything else and it makes it *very* hard to learn new things. It makes it hard to even admit that it would be a good idea to learn new things and you certainly won't ever admit to feeling unconfident. Gurus set themselves up as being good, excellent, possibly the only ones who can do what they do and that is an impossible expectation to live up to. Because there are hundreds, maybe thousands of people out there who can teach as well as them. The fact is, that although we are unique as human beings, and we may offer a unique combination of approaches, the likelihood is that there are *many* others out there just as good as us. However, if you look to this sort of hero worship for your self-validation then your self esteem will be false, you start feeling insecure, leading to lack of flexibility, rigidity and the absence of an open mind. Spare a thought for people trapped in that cycle of certainty and denial, trying to live up to that impossible expectation.

There are some coaches you meet who are open minded, open to new ideas and new approaches, while still being very sure of themselves. These people are sure that they have something of value to offer and they can listen to you, hear your story and come up with ideas to help you specifically on your journey. These are the ones who have true confidence, and if you say anything to them to try to give them guru status they will most likely laugh and knock that idea right down.

So, why is The Guru Syndrome a problem? Well it's fairly obvious from this side of things: someone who has fallen victim to The Guru Syndrome will not be good for *your* confidence! They will be giving you the answers, tools and techniques *they* would use, they will be telling rather than listening and you will not get the knowledge and information you need for *your* journey. Instead they will be trying to get you to go on their journey, and that is not good for your confidence!

Now let's look at the other side of the coin: because this is human nature too: what about when students or coaches try to give guru status to their teacher or coach, whether they want it or not? What's going on here? Why is it a bad thing to admire your coach or teacher so much? This is actually quite a common thing: if you find someone who seems to explain things it's only natural to ascribe positive thoughts to them.

There is in fact a well known psychological event called 'The Halo Effect' where when someone is good at one thing, it is human nature to start passing that positive feeling onto other areas of their lives. So when we meet someone who can explain things in a way we can understand, help us be better at something we are struggling with, it's only natural to start thinking of them in a totally positive, non critical way and start to assign guru status to them. The heroes we choose, and a guru is a form of hero, really are the people who have attributes *we* would like to have and who have things we aspire to having or being. Having a hero to inspire us, to aspire to emulate, is a good thing. It motivates us to keep learning, keep practising. However, when we start giving them guru status, something changes. It stops being a good thing and starts being very bad for us.

How? Well, I can use an example. Someone recently decided to try to give me guru status. She said, "You are so wonderful, the only person who really understands what is going on with me and my issues.". On the one hand, that was lovely to hear, great for my ego. That was the clue for me: whenever I feel my ego basking, I know it's time to take a closer look! After all, coaching isn't supposed to be about me. It's supposed to be about the person I am with—it's *their* journey.

So when someone tries to make it about me, what is happening? Well, by making it about me and how good *I* am, they are in fact downgrading their own contribution and making it harder for themselves to believe that they can do it too. In many ways they are abdicating their responsibility to learn. After all, if I have some mystical gift, which they don't have, then they can't be expected to learn what I have learned. They can keep muddling along without that gift, and nothing will change. So when you assign guru status to a coach or instructor, you are actually abdicating responsibility for your own learning and progress. That means that any confidence you feel or get is only because you are confident in your coach, not in yourself. So you will only be confident when you are around that instructor or their representatives and you will not be developing your *own* confidence at all. This isn't sustainable confidence because as soon as that instructor or coach leaves you not only have no confidence, you also have no tools with which to build your own confidence. And that is certainly not good for you.

Now, when people say, "Wow, that was amazing, how can I learn to do that too?", *this* is when we are talking healthy hero stuff. Seeing that someone can do things because they have learned them leads to the belief that we can too, and that is the foundation for building a constructive plan to move forward.

In closing: it's good to have heroes. I have many I meet everyday. People I admire and emulate, people I take some ideas from and try to make my own. Without heroes I would be very uninspired and probably uninspiring.

However, in our Confidence Journey, we can do without gurus. We need to take responsibility for our own learning, and not abdicate it, which leaves us and our lives in a worse place than we were before.

Who are *your* heroes who inspire and motivate you?
How can you make sure *you* don't fall victim to The Guru Syndrome?

## Trap 5

## Faux amis: False friends, when confidence may not be what it seems

When you learn a foreign language, there comes a stage when you learn about 'faux amis'. Literally translated, this means 'false friends' and in language learning, this refers to phrases or words which sound easy to translate, but are in fact not that straightforward. For example, many words in English and French come from the same roots, and so mean the same thing and appear similar. Amiable (English) and aimable (French) look similar and mean the same thing. However, many are similar, but mean very *different* things. For example:

Extra means 'plus' or 'in addition' in English. In French the same word *also* means 'outstanding' or 'special'.

'Miserable' means sad in English, but means 'shabby, run down' in French. Here is a big one: in English 'inhabited' means someone lives there. In French 'inhabite' means *no-one* lives there!

What on earth does this have to do with confidence? Well, this can happen with confidence too. Something that looks like confidence, can often be mistaken for confidence when in fact, it is not. This can happen when we are with friends, and we think they are confident because they act that way, when actually we have no idea of how they are really feeling on the inside. Or it can happen when we trick ourselves. We trick ourselves into thinking we are better than we really are, that we know more—and that we are more confident than we really are. Why on earth would we do this?

Remember, our unconscious just wants us to stay safe and being happy is being safe from sadness, so it may allow us to pretend to be confident in order to be happy about ourselves. Think about it. One of the hardest things for anyone to do is to be happy with themselves, warts and all. We all want some positive thing to hold onto and being unconfident can be a really negative place to be. The appeal of finding confidence can be seductive and so when one thing works, we tell ourselves, "Look we are ok, we are confident now.", and that can lead to some challenges.

Anthony had worked hard on his Confidence Journey, with the goal of being able to lead a key project at work while staying within his Confidence Zone. He had been through the IDEAS Process in step 3, calculated his WHAT IFs and come up with a Graphic Visualisation plan that inspired and motivated him. Then he led a project at work and it all came together in a great way. He immediately emailed me to say, "I'm confident again! I don't need to do this stuff anymore!".

What happened next? He took the confidence from that one project to mean he was fully confident, so stopped using the tools, stopped paying attention to how he was feeling and things seemed to be going just fine for the next few weeks.

Recently he got in touch again. He realised that he had let himself be carried away by the excitement of that first, confident, project. Much to his surprise, after just one more successful project, he found himself losing his confidence again, this time worse than before. Luckily he noticed this and worked out that in his eagerness to 'be fixed' and to 'be confident' he had tricked himself into thinking that one good project meant he was all ok. Therefore when the next project came along, he had not stopped to check his confidence thresholds, had missed the early signs of not being in his Confidence Zone, and had ended up pushing himself repeatedly through his confidence thresholds ultimately leading to the current loss of confidence. He had confused the feelings of success with confidence, and actually ended up with 'false confidence'. Interestingly, the word 'false friends' came into play in another way for him. He said his friends were so relieved he had found his confidence that they refused to accept he was anything less than 'cured' and that had also contributed to the relapse.

One way of testing whether your confidence after doing something is authentic or false is to apply the 'phew/yay' test. It is a simple test: if, after doing the activity you walk away going, "Phew, I survived!", then that most likely means you were outside your Confidence Zone when doing it. If however, you walk away feeling, "Yay, that felt great and I still feel great.", than that is most likely authentic confidence. One caveat on this test—it doesn't always work if you are on a real adrenalin high, as that gives you a 'yay' response however scared you were, so we need to watch out for that!

This goes back to some fundamental concepts. First, confidence isn't an object you lose, then find. It isn't something that you have in your pocket and it can fall out. Second, confidence isn't 'who you are.'. It is not your identity. You are not a 'confident person' or an 'unconfident person'. Third, confidence isn't always knowing exactly what to do and how to do it or knowing what will work and what won't. What *is* confidence? *Real* confidence, as opposed to the false friend of confidence we often hold onto?

> *"Confidence is a belief that whatever happens in that particular situation, you know how to be safe: physically, emotionally and mentally."* Cathy Sirett, Confidence Coach

How can we help ourselves avoid this trap? Largely it is about having a certain mindset. If we have a fixed mindset, where we see ourselves as in a fixed state, which may be flawed but can be 'fixed' and 'returned to functionality' then this leads us towards this trap. If however, we have a 'growth' mindset we are less vulnerable to this.

What is a growth mindset? It's seeing ourselves as we really are, as a constant work in progress, never perfect, never complete and always able to learn and develop more. Interestingly, in any path of spirituality or religion, it is often said that the hardest thing for any human to do is to accept themselves as they truly are. For me, to realise I am always a beginner, always learning, always imperfect and that I often have to work hard to find a way to be confident in a situation means I am accepting myself as an imperfect flawed human being. This isn't easy. It means that when something I was scared about turns out well I don't just check the box and say, "Great, that part of me is now fixed.", and move on. It means I look at that as progress, and learn from the experience to see what I need to do now to sustain that confidence and progress, and perhaps even move further along in my Confidence Journey.

For most of us it's not easy to maintain a growth mindset. Most of us either ignore our flaws, or spiral into a pit of despair at how terrible we are. Neither of these are helpful. We need to find a space between those two points of view. We need to find the place where we are not perfect, we are not right and we are not wrong. A place where we are working on being as good a 'me' as we can be right now, with the resources we have available. This book is sharing resources with you to expand what you can do. We need to find a place where we are allowed to be learners; we are allowed to be beginners; we are allowed to not know what we are doing. Hopefully we know how to stay safe while we are playing around and trying to work this out.

Only when we can see ourselves as we really are, can we start to work on becoming who we want to be. False friends, and false confidence: watch out for them, and don't let them take you away from who you really are. Allow yourself to be worthy of the truth.

Those are the five main confidence traps I see on a regular basis. There are more but these are the ones that consistently make a difference to the people I work with. With that many traps you might think that the whole area of confidence is a minefield, and it is. Luckily though, I have also come across five Tips that will accelerate your Confidence Journey safely and significantly.

# CONFIDENCE JOURNEY ACCELERATOR TIPS

## Tip 1
### Know yourself: What's your blind spot?

I had three clients who at first sight seemed to be focusing on three different issues. However, after meeting them all there were some significant commonalities across the three. First let me summarise the issues they were focusing on:

1. Sandra: My own impatience is causing me to push my team at work through their confidence thresholds, leading to more conflict than there should be and to me being perceived as 'bullying' them at times.

2. Emma: I don't trust my team members to do their share of the work on this project to the right standard, so I am finding it hard to delegate.

3. Rachel: I have a great team, I can rely on them and they all know their stuff. But I am still not delegating

to them, I am still micromanaging them and not letting them get on with their roles. This is becoming a major issue for them and I need to stop doing it!

As I said, we could look at each one of these as a separate issue. However, if we think about it, there is one thing they all share and that is the leaders' confidence in themselves and their ability to trust their teams.

In the first one, Sandra's eagerness to make progress means she misses the moments when her team members hesitate, or she doesn't hear them when they express their doubts and concerns. This means they end up being pushed through these concerns and worries. They push themselves through their own concerns and then react badly later when yet another stress point or threshold is crossed. In other words Sandra is not seeing the 'trigger stacking' in her team. Trigger stacking is where each time a threshold is crossed, the anxiety level is raised until on the sixth or seventh trigger the anxiety becomes unbearable and the person explodes or breaks down. It explains the 'straw that broke the camel's back' saying, as the first triggers often go un-noticed by others and the resulting explosion comes as a complete surprise to them.

In the second situation, Emma is not sure how to handle the 'WHAT IFs' that keep crowding into her mind, which is making it hard to relax and trust her team. In the third case, despite knowing her team is capable and competent, Rachel has discovered that the real issue is she doesn't trust herself and her ability to delegate.

Each of these is about how we manage ourselves, and our mind, thoughts and behaviour, particularly with respect to our teams.

The good thing about all three of these statements is that their owners are aware they each have an issue: self awareness is a pre-requisite for self management so the first steps have been taken. Until you know there is a problem, how can you even begin to look for solutions?

The path to self awareness can be challenging: for Rachel, realising that it is about her has been a shock. For Sandra, acknowledging that it is her own impatience putting her and her team's performance at risk is a scary thing. To accept that you don't trust your team because of your own mind's patterns can be difficult. This is why a coach or objective friend can be so helpful: they can reflect what they see, and you can compare it with what you *think* you are doing—and this helps you become aware of where the images don't match.

The Johari Window is a tool used in management training that has some bearing here. It was created in 1955 by two psychologists, Joseph Luft and Harrington Ingham. The name "Johari" comes from combining their two first names. There are many versions, each with slightly different wording. Here is the one I like to use:

## JOHARI WINDOW

|  | KNOWN TO SELF | UNKNOWN TO SELF |
|---|---|---|
| KNOWN TO OTHERS | PUBLIC SELF | BLIND SPOT |
| UNKNOWN TO OTHERS | PRIVATE SELF | INVISIBLE SELF |

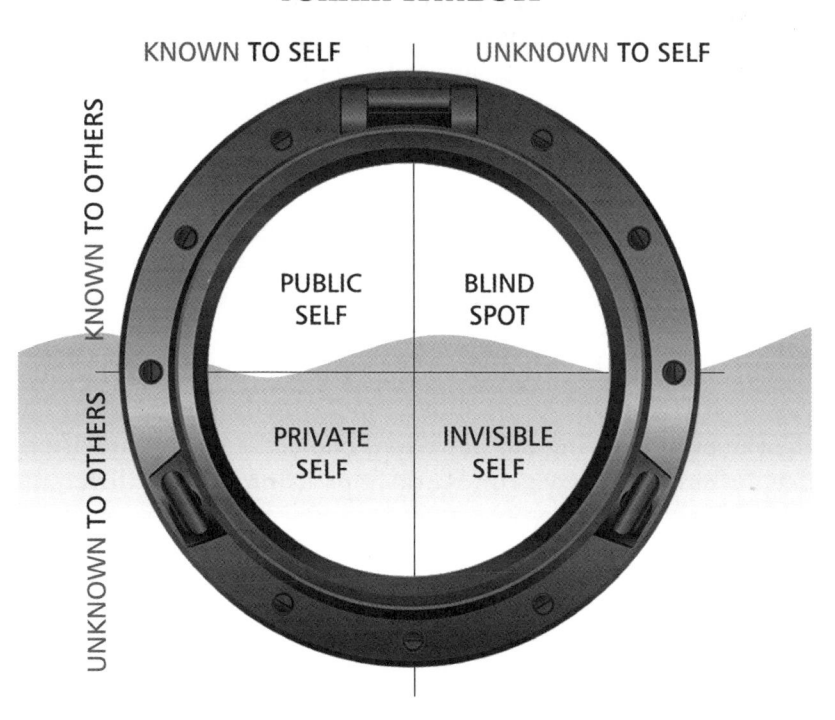

There are aspects of ourselves that we are aware of, some of which we choose to share with others (the Public self) and some of which we don't (the Private self). Then there are aspects of ourselves that we are not aware of. These are things we don't know and others don't know either (the Invisible self) and things that others are aware of, but we are not (the Blind Spot). Self awareness in general will move that central dividing line to the right, increasing the Private and Public selves and reducing the Invisible self and Blind Spot. The more awareness we have, the more choices we have, more choices usually means more control and more control leads to more confidence. It all starts with self awareness. How can you increase your self awareness? The obvious one is to tackle the Blind Spot. Talk to people (or rather, listen to them), hear what they say and see how that can help you become more aware of yourself.

As a specific example, I posted on an online forum recently and triggered a rather strong negative response. I could take that a few different ways: I could ignore it and say, "They don't know what they're talking about!"; I could take it very personally and get angry and defensive, or I could stop for a moment and reflect on what might be leading to that response, and see what I can learn from it to increase my awareness, choices and control in the future. That's why even coaches use coaches: by having someone else observe and feed back, we can make that blind spot smaller and smaller.

There is another way to increase self awareness—we can change the size of the Invisible self too: psychological inventories can highlight aspects of ourselves that even our closest friends don't know about, especially those that focus on the values underlying our behaviour choices, as values are often deeply hidden. I have run workshops using several different inventories and tools where in almost every case, even working with groups of family members or very close friends, more of the Invisible self is revealed.

There are some things that block self awareness, which if we know about them, make it easier to move past them. I am sure we have all heard of denial, but what lies behind that? One concept that is particularly useful here is that of 'secondary gain'.

Secondary gain is the positive benefit the mind perceives as a result of a behaviour or action and is often unconscious. So if I 'feel happier' thinking I *am* confident, then I might be in denial about any indicators to the contrary. Secondary gain can also be about avoiding a negative, so if admitting I was unconfident would have a horrific impact on me then I will stay in denial to avoid that emotional trauma. For example, if I train horses and say I am unconfident then what on earth could happen to my life?

In Sandra's case, it is possible that if she did take the time to recognise her team's thresholds, she would discover how many they have, how many she has been pushing them through, how close she has come to being a bully, which would be unbearably upsetting for her to realise. Thinking, "They will be ok.", is much easier in the moment. It could also be that part of her identity is currently being an 'impulsive extrovert' and slowing down enough to take the time it takes is something that threatens this identity. In both these cases, some time spent with a coach could work through this and get to the secondary gain and help Sandra decide how to manage this for herself. Some people manage to coach themselves through this, and I hope that sharing the information in this tip post will help some of you do exactly that. Once you have identified the 'parts' of you that are not congruent, or working together you can use the process described in the 'Confidence Kidnappers' chapter in Part 2 to bring the two elements together so instead of fighting yourself, you are using all your parts to move forward in the same direction.

When I hear someone speak and think that they are in denial, I ask myself, "What is that denial doing for them? What is the positive intent of that denial?", and that helps me understand their world, and how to work with that world rather than against it. By doing this I know that any results of a coaching session will fit with their overall ecology and be sustainable over the long term.

By being aware of your Johari Window, and the concept of secondary gain, you can significantly accelerate your Confidence Journey.

## Tip 2
## Know yourself: Who's in control?

One of the things that can happen on our Confidence Journey is we get knocked back by other things happening in life. If we have a way of recovering from these knocks quickly and effectively, then this accelerates our Confidence Journey towards positive results. This tip focuses on how we can build our resilience when things don't go to plan.

Many people go on workshops or courses and come away inspired with confidence, and indeed feel confident and relaxed for quite some time. Then, one thing happens, they have a bad experience, and suddenly the nerves are back. What is happening here is that whilst the surface issues of confidence are being addressed, the underlying foundation for confidence is not being solidly constructed. This can be for many reasons: it might be that there are other things in your life that affect you, so even though one side of things is sorted, the rest of your life is not, and as time goes on this comes back into your mind and erodes your confidence from the course or workshop.

It might be that the course *did* sort out your confidence but now something *new* is affecting it and you don't have the tools and strategies to deal with this new thing.

It might be that in the excitement of feeling confident again, you have pushed yourself through some of your own thresholds, ignoring your inner voice saying, "Be careful!". Then your unconscious has to frighten you to get your attention back and make you careful again!

It could be for many reasons, which is why it's important that each one of us understands about confidence, how to build it, and how to access our own toolkit with tools ready-to-use when things don't quite go as planned.

Having a Confidence Journey with a toolkit, and knowing how to use the tools, is one key aspect of having sustainable confidence, of being resilient. After all, if we have a flat tyre, but know how to change it then it is less of a big deal than if we don't have the tools or knowledge.

However, there is something even more fundamental that affects our ability to build sustainable confidence, or resilience, and that is a facet of ourselves that can make it harder or easier to be resilient: whether we have an external or internal locus of control.

A 'locus of control' is where we see control of our lives. If I have an external locus of control, then I tend to believe that everything that controls my life is *outside* me, and therefore outside my control. Someone with an external locus of control, when they are late to work will say, "Ah, well the traffic was bad; what could I do?". If I have an *internal* locus of control, then I tend to believe that everything that controls my life is *inside* me, and therefore within my control. Someone with an internal locus of control, when they are late to work will say' "Ah, the traffic was bad; I should have left earlier.".

See the difference?

There are a few things to know about this locus of control concept before we get carried away using it for anything.

1. If we look at the population as a whole, we will see that there tends to be a distribution with a pretty wide spread.

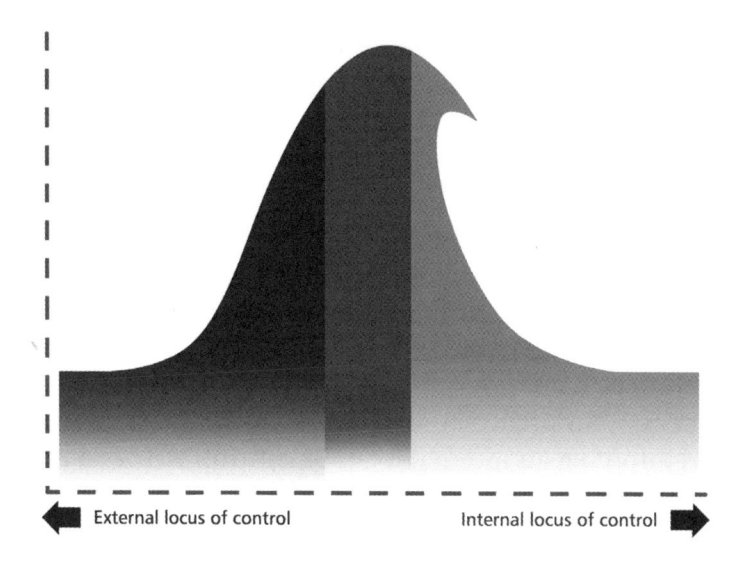

⬅ External locus of control　　　Internal locus of control ➡

Most people will fit in the middle where their locus of control isn't very extreme.

2. For those in the middle of this curve, our locus of control can vary depending on the situation. When I am dealing with bureaucracy, for example a recent interaction with the expenses approval system in a large corporation, I know I am not in control! Therefore in that situation my locus of control is external and rightly so. However, I will tend to inhabit a place where I am more external or internal most of the time. With my recent run-in with bureaucracy while I couldn't control what was happening, and the apparently unending requests for filling out yet more paperwork, I *could* control how I felt about it. I could choose whether to go around ranting and raving and feeling angry or I could choose, using the self management skills I have learned over the years, to step back from it, accept it as how it is and make the best of things.

3. This is the key: for 99% of us, our locus of control is learned and therefore *changeable*.

Think about five-year olds in school. What if we were to keep track of how many comments a child received in a day that reinforced an internal or external locus of control? Comments that reinforced an external locus of control would be if they were playing with blocks and the blocks fell down, "Oh never mind, the blocks are uneven, no wonder they fell down.". An internal locus of control comment in this same scenario would be, "Look, if you put the blocks like *this* then they will stay up!". Can you guess how many external and internal locus of control comments the five-year old would get? In one story shared in a workshop, one teacher said she noticed that in one day at her school one child got almost 200 comments reinforcing an external locus of control, and only nine reinforcing an internal locus of control? A friend of mine used to stop her child from crying when he fell or banged into things by slapping the offending pavement or table and saying,

"Bad pavement, bad table.". It made them laugh and stopped the tears but it also started building a strongly external locus of control in her little boy, where he started blaming objects and other people when things didn't go as he wanted. When she shifted gears to emphasising more internal comments, she noticed a significant change in his behaviours and decisions.

I know from my own experience that this is changeable. I grew up a highly internally focused person, and my first job as a sales rep for a major pharmaceutical company was going well. I was speaking at the national conference on how I had achieved the highest ever sales growth in the company in my first nine months on the territory. All this progress was before a new manager came on board and within three months I was an externally focused person thinking nothing was in my control. Thank goodness I left that job and found my balance again, but it was proof to me that locus of control *is* changeable.

Think about it for a minute: what are the kinds of things that cause you to believe things are out of your control (i.e. they will move you to the left on the curve)? Some things might include: being told what to do; being told of all your mistakes with no tools to help you correct them; not knowing how to predict a situation (e.g. not being able to read your team); not knowing how to fix things (e.g. what can I do to calm down conflict with people); doing things mechanically, by rote, rather than understanding them. What others can you think of?

What kind of things will move you to the right; to a more internal locus? Maybe: knowledge, tools, techniques, knowing you have all of these, having support, knowing others who have dealt with the same situation? All of these things will increase your capacity to feel that you *can* manage things, you *can* control them. It's just a matter of learning *how* to.

Why does this matter? Well, if we have an external focus about our confidence, it is easily knocked. If our confidence depends on external things which we have no control over, then the slightest thing will set us back as we will not believe we have the resources to sort things out. If we have an internal focus, then when there is a set back, instead of saying, "It was my boss' fault, it was the weather, it was the situation...", we can say, "Hmm, looks like I don't know how to manage my boss effectively, how to cope when the weather changes, or how to handle these situations...yet. I had better find a way to learn...". In the first example, there is nothing you can do to change things. In the second, it might be a lot of effort and take some time but it *can* be done. Which one is better for sustainable confidence?

One last thing about locus of control: it is possible to be *too* internally focused. Yes, seriously, it is: when you are *too* internally focused, you take responsibility for everything and this can start what is called a 'neurotic spiral' which goes something like this: "It's my fault I can't do this; I am no good in this role; I shouldn't be doing this what on earth made me think I could;, I'm just bringing everyone else down; I should just give up and then everyone else would be better off without me.". I think we all go there now and then. The trouble is if we stay there, it is very hard to get out again and it's a very miserable place to be unless you have good friends and family to help.

For sustainable confidence to be resilient in the face of challenges and changes, we need to do two things. First, identify what the challenge is and second, turn it into something where we can ask these questions: "How can I manage this with confidence? What *can* I do to feel more confident here?". A recent example is a friend of mine who had her horse started by a very good horseman, and rode happily when on the handover workshop but then got home and realised she was very worried about her horse's reactions to her now she was alone. While she was focused on the worry and what she hadn't got control of (e.g. I have no instructor here, no one to help me if things go wrong, I can't control my horse's excitement and energy) she felt horrible and 'stuck'. When she refocused and asked herself, "Well, I know all that but what *can* I do to feel more confident here?", she came up with several answers including:

I can do a few days of groundwork in the arena and field to just remind myself that I *can* do things by myself.

I can make a point of sticking to the plans I make—that will help my unconscious to trust me.

I can do a lot of saddling and mounting practice with a lot of on and off so I can prove to myself my horse is ok with me on him.

I can break things down and do them small steps at a time and check I am below a 5 at each stage on my Confidence Score and check my *horse* is below a 5 at each stage too.

I can use patterns to help us both relax make things predictable but with a few obstacles now and then to keep him interested.

Here's what she said after this conversation:
"Once I had a list of things I *could* do to stay confident, it was like a weight lifting off my shoulders. Instead of focusing on what I couldn't do, I had stacks of things I could do and that changed things completely! Since this discussion I have been making huge progress in my confidence and Hannibal and I are back to where we were at the handover workshop, but we are doing it ourselves."

We can't always change the facts—what we *can* change is what we *do* about the facts.

Steven Covey, in his powerful book 'The seven habits of highly effective people', talks of people creating their 'circles of concern', in which they place everything they are worried about with respect to a particular issue. He then directs people to place another circle inside that one, called a 'circle of influence' where they look at all the concerns and leave anything they can't influence, and focus on everything they *can* influence. One point he makes is that most of us consistently underestimate what we *can* influence and that the more we can put inside that circle, the more we are empowered and in control of our lives.

I was working with a team who had a lot of anxiety about some organisational changes that were in the pipeline but had not been finalised. One of the biggest areas of concern was who would be their line manager after the changes, as they had been with their current line manager for five years. At first the team had nothing in their circle of influence as they could only see that they had no control here. However, when I challenged them as to what they *could* control they realised that they knew it would be one of three people, and so they could research and identify constructive plans to reduce anxiety whoever became their manager. They identified actions such as talking to people currently being managed by these three, working out how to interact effectively with them, planning their initial conversations with each of the three to 'fit' with each manager's style and preferences—so there was a lot they could see themselves doing to take more control. As they realised this, you could see the tension level in the room dropping. Identifying what we *can* control has a large impact.

Focusing and developing our locus of control can significantly accelerate our Confidence Journey!

# Tip 3

## Know yourself: How to be mindful—and why it matters to our confidence

Did you know there is a difference between adrenalin-based learning and enjoyment, and endorphin-based learning and enjoyment?

Adrenalin is the 'fight or flight' hormone: when we feel stressed, frightened, anxious or excited, it's adrenalin that floods through our body causing us to feel that intense flush of tension. Our airways open and our smoother muscles get ready to run or act. The lining of our arterioles actually contracts and changes our blood flow to our muscles. We feel this when we have a 'near miss' when driving, or in a scary situation such as when we bungee jump or skydive. Interestingly, we feel this when we are excited too.

Even more interestingly, adrenalin, unlike most other neuro-transmitters in the body, does not regulate itself. With most chemicals as they fill the body, systems act to reduce them again and restore the balance. Since adrenalin is a 'survival' chemical—giving us that extra strength to run or fight, there is no such system in place for this, so the 'buzz' lasts a long time.

Ever heard the phrase 'adrenalin junkie'? Thrill seeker? People who do things because of the 'buzz' they get from doing them? There are a lot of those around in almost every area of life. People who finish a presentation and as they come out of the room say, "Thank goodness that is over! I did it!". People who get back from a ride on their horses and say, "Phew! I survived!" are on an adrenalin high of living through what was for them a frightening experience. We all know people who live on adrenalin: people who come out of a meeting feeling they have 'beaten' everyone else in the room; people who get a kick out of controlling the conversation and winning the argument. Their cheeks are flushed, they are warm, excited and thrilled to have won; they have overcome and achieved their high.

And while this buzz lasts, this adrenalin high can be a great thing to experience. When we bungee jump, skydive or even just survive a driving mistake, it can be a great feeling. Some people get addicted to it and become 'adrenalin junkies'. Basically, they are constantly seeking out that 'high' which is caused by self-inducing a fight-or-flight response by intentionally engaging in stressful or risky behaviour, which causes a release of epinephrine by the adrenal gland. Adrenalin junkies appear to deliberately choose stressful activities for the release of epinephrine as a stress response.

However, there is another set of chemicals in our body that also produce a great feeling after stressful events; endorphins, also released during the fight-or-flight response to such activities. Endorphins belong to the opiate family. They give us that lovely relaxed feeling of wellbeing that we get after the stress is over, when our body is flooded with good feelings. An endorphin rush is qualitatively different to an adrenalin rush. The latter leaves you sharp, on edge, ready to run or fight, a 'bring it on!' or 'make my day' kind of feeling. The former leaves you glowing, bathing in sunlight, warm and fuzzy whilst still thinking clearly. A very pleasant feeling with an accompanying clarity of mind. There is a reason why opiates are generally addictive when taken as drugs.

Here's the thing: if you have any form of confidence issue, the chances are that you are operating on adrenalin for at least part of the time. The flight or fight response is triggered, you feel tense, sharp, on edge. Super aware of everything and ready to react at the slightest thing. You're on a hair trigger with a direct line to predator-level.

It's not very enjoyable to feel like that around people, is it? Yet having an urgent project when you are unsure and unconfident, or having a meeting where you know you will be measured and assessed for your contribution can put you right in that adrenalin zone. Quite often we put ourselves there because, in our experience, triggering the high adrenalin state is the way to get things done. Or, we might recognise the sharpness of our feelings and emotions and do something else: we might bottle it all up, push it down inside and pretend it's not there. The thing is, it *is* there. And it is a genuine chemical response to our fear or anxiety. Denying it doesn't change a thing. We still have a body full of adrenalin, and will be thinking and moving in ways that will not help our relationship with our team—and so we will end up becoming even more unconfident.

When we are full of adrenalin or even have just a slight layer sitting there, our heart rate increases, our movements will be sharper, our voice and tone will be louder, we will be faster to tense and subconsciously, other people notice this and they start getting on edge too. We lose the ability to have that measured thoughtful approach that gives us the time to really notice what is happening with our team and make better quality decisions. It's not all in our mind. It's a by-product of a chemical in our body. All part of our evolutionary development.

What happens in the endorphin state?

When we are in the endorphin state, we feel alive, energised—but in a different way. Time appears to slow, we feel warm, connected, and our whole body moves in a more fluid way. Our heart rate might speed up but it can slow down as well. Endorphins are released with the stress of physical exercise, but also when we relax and meditate. Interestingly, the 'flow' state that is said to lead to high quality performance is considered an endorphin state. So what does someone in an endorphin state look like?

Ever had that feeling of being 'in the moment'? When time stretches forever and yet it seems just a moment since you started and you are amazed at how much time has actually passed? Ever felt that 'sigh' of relaxation when something finally clicks into place? Ever finished a meeting and felt a glow about how smoothly it all went?

Think about how this state affects how you are when you are around other people. When people are in the adrenalin state, they will be tight, aggressive, fearful and focused on control and winning. When people are in the endorphin state they will be relaxed, open, calm, and focused on being in the moment and accepting what happens, flowing with it.

Which one is better for confidence?

Almost everything we do in our lives can be done in either state. Think about it: we can go to the beach for the thrill or for the gallop, the danger of not knowing if we will stay on, if our horse will go in the water, for the massive rush we will get and remember when we tell the story later about how scared we really were and how we overcame it. Or, we can go to the beach and glory in how relaxed we both are, how our horse looks to us for confidence and guidance and how we can softly canter in the waves on a loose rein...

We can go to a meeting with fire in our belly and ready for battle, the rush of not knowing what will happen, and the buzz we get when it's over and we won! Or, we can get into a flow state and be amazed at how easily the meeting goes, how everyone is working together, and how straightforward it was to get everything done. I know which one I prefer.

Ok, so it's all very well saying we are better off in an endorphin state, but how on earth do we GET there?

Here are some ideas that will help us:

1. *Never do anything when you are over a 5*

We have talked before about scoring your Confidence Zone. Anything below 5 means you are confident enough to do it safely, without any doubt, although you might have to think a bit. Anything above a 5 brings stress, tension and so encourages the adrenalin state. If you know you are going to stay below a 5, how much easier is it to relax and be open to the endorphin state instead?

2. *Breathe*

Take deep breaths. In fact take five deep breaths and focus on each of your senses for one breath. This grounds you in the moment, and is the easiest and most basic form of mindfulness and meditation.

3. *Be mindful*

This is the key to being in the endorphin state versus the adrenalin state: the art of being *mindful*.

One of my favourite writers/philosopher is Michel de Montaigne (born 1533). He was a French essayist in the Renaissance. In fact, he developed a unique essay style, much discussed at the time and admired later where he directly engaged his personal experiences into his thinking about life, the universe and everything. He is particularly famous for one essay which contains four words that became his motto, "What do I know?". He was famously sceptical of everything—explored how people thought and lived and while not seeing himself as a philosopher, ended up being viewed as one of the most influential thinkers of the time. His influence can, for example, be seen in many of Shakespeare's plays and he was a renowned negotiator of conciliations between warring factions. My favourite story of Montaigne's is one where he tells the take of an Ancient Greek philosopher talking to a king.

The philosopher asks: "What are you going to do now?"
King: "I'm going to conquer Italy"
Philosopher: "What are you going to do after that?"
King: "I'm going to conquer Africa"
Philosopher: "What are you going to do after that?"
King: "I'm going to conquer the world!"
Philosopher: "And what are you going to do after that?"
King: "I'm going to sit down, have glass of wine and relax…"

To which the philosopher replies, "Why don't you just sit down *now* and have a glass of wine and relax?"

Montaigne's view was why go on doing all those things that are about becoming important if all that really matters is sitting down having a glass of wine relaxing and being at peace with yourself? And so to Montaigne, the whole enterprise of life is one of learning how to live with yourself, and you can only do that if you learn to escape from some of these anxieties and vanities that drive you.

Sometimes we are so focused on what we need to do to become important that we forget why we are doing a lot of these things: to make us happy either directly (having fun, doing our hobbies and pastimes) or indirectly (earning money that will enable us to enjoy life). As humans we are often so focused on the past, or the future that we forget that to truly enjoy life we need to think about being in the moment and enjoying the now. This is where practicing mindfulness can help: practicing mindfulness gives us the skills we need to be able to access the endorphin state 'on demand'.

So a tip to accelerate your Confidence Journey is to develop the skill of being in an endorphin state through mindfulness and flow. I mentioned one simple exercise earlier in this tip: take five breaths and for each breath, focus on one of your five senses. What can you taste? What can you smell? What can you hear? What can you see? What can you feel? This is a mindfulness activity that takes less than a minute and yet centres you in your own body and in the here and now. An extended version of this exercise is to repeat it but focus on each sense for five breaths. Mindfulness can be as simple as that. There is a great blog called 'The Mindfulness Journey' on Wordpress that is a 100-day journey to mindfulness for people who find it hard to meditate. There are also some great apps that can help you develop your mindfulness.

There are some links, resources and ideas for this on the website cathysirett.com in the Complete Confidence section.

## Tip 4
## Be grateful: The attitude of gratitude

We have already seen that being thankful to fear is a powerful way of achieving a partnership that keeps you safe and allows you to achieve your goals. Something as simple as saying 'thank You' can radically change your relationships with your work colleagues, your friends, your horse and yourself.

Interesting, isn't it? Just saying those two words can lead to totally different dynamics between us, and yet many of us don't realise this. Saying 'thank you' to someone changes how that person perceives you, and how they feel about you. If you do a search on gratitude you will find it is becoming increasingly popular in organisations as an effective business tool. Let's take a look at this, and the impact it has with our horses, our work colleagues and friends and ourselves.

*With our horses:*

Most of us like to be nice to our horses. When we are with them we often say 'good boy' or 'good girl' and pat or stroke them when things go well. So here's a question for you: What is the difference for you and your horse when you say 'thank you' vs when you say 'good boy'? If you think about that, or even take a moment to go to your horse and try this, you will notice there are some rather large differences. When we say 'good boy' (or girl) we say it as praise, as a congratulations for doing something well or right, which immediately means some form of judgement is involved. While this isn't necessarily a bad thing, it is still a judgement, an assessment—and can be heard as such. 'Good boy' can mean you did that right, you accomplished the task, I am pleased with you, you have pleased me. It is a more direct line, outcome-related upward energy. When we say 'thank-you', we say it as a release, a softening. An acknowledgement that we have received a gift or offering. Thank you can mean very different things to 'good boy'. It is a being-related, downward energy.

Try this with your horse: when he offers you something great, or something you appreciate say 'thank you' . You will notice your energy is different, your emotional state is different—and you will also notice your horse's response will be different.

*With our colleagues and friends:*

Sometimes it's hard to say 'thank you'. But it makes a huge difference. How many times have you stopped at a zebra crossing (for those of you not in the UK these are road crossings for pedestrians which are not controlled by lights, so rely on drivers 'agreeing' to follow the road rules and stop to let people cross) and watched people cross and they haven't even acknowledged you? How did you feel? And how do you feel when they *do* give you a little nod or wave to say 'thank you'? There's a big difference...

When someone says 'thank you' it creates a positive emotional state in both people in the exchange, the thanker and the thankee—and that changes how people view each other. Research shows that people thanked for their behaviours are more inclined to offer more supportive and altruistic behaviours, and become more positive in how they view others; whereas those who are not thanked tend to reduce their offerings, and also become more negative about the people they interact with. For more information on some of this research, head over to the website where there are some references and links to relevant articles.

Two simple words that can make such massive changes in how people respond to you, and how eager they are to help you. Remember though, that like anything, it has to be authentic. The effort with gratitude comes in identifying something you can genuinely say thank you for, because any sense of 'fake' in your thank you will negate any positive impact and most likely have the opposite effect to the one you want.

When working as a consultant in business, a lot of my management coaching is focused on enabling managers to identify behaviours and actions they can be genuinely thankful for, with authenticity. This has made a huge difference to many of them in how their teams respond to them and how they feel about their teams.

Interestingly there are also differences in the people who were *doing* the thanking: people who say thank you more often are generally happier, more relaxed, more positive in their outlook and the simple act of saying 'thank you' triggers a positive emotional state in us.

This can be *very* useful.

One of the things about working with confidence is that often, there are lots of people who suddenly know what we should be doing, and how we should be doing it. In fact, this is true of most of the business world! This can get annoying, and I know it is easy to end up in a very negative state about all this advice. We often get to the stage where we avoid people, or end up arguing with them – which takes an awful lot of energy and isn't pleasant for us *or* them. So—what if we just said 'thank you'...?

I was in an office once where I was the only person using a particular approach to planning my work. It was based on mind mapping rather than the spreadsheet based planning most people there were used to. Not surprisingly, everyone had advice on what I should be doing and how I should be planning. I started listening to their advice, waiting until they finished talking then simply smiling and saying 'thank you'. In my heart I was thanking them for the time and effort they were putting into their well-intentioned efforts to help me do what they thought was best. And something interesting happened.

The interactions became softer, more positive. On both sides. As people saw me listen and heard my thank you they relaxed, became less pushy about their points of view and the whole dynamic changed. Monologues became conversations and my time at the office became a lot more enjoyable. This was great for *my* confidence too. Instead of feeling under pressure to do things differently, I was able to continue in my own way without pressure or stress, and without having to argue with anyone. All because all I had to say was 'thank you' I felt differently about things too. What a difference.

*With ourselves:*

I have talked before in this book about how to handle fear, and negotiating with our unconscious to help us find our true confidence. Here is the first thing to do whenever you notice you are feeling unconfident, worried or anxious about anything: Say 'thank you'. Really. As you are driving down the road to your office, and you feel those butterflies starting to flutter around in your stomach: say 'Thank you'. Thank you for wanting to keep me safe, and make sure I pay attention to myself and my safety.

That is all your unconscious is doing when it causes you to feel fear or worry or to 'lose' your confidence: it's just trying to keep you safe. That is a wonderful thing. To know that a part of you is always looking out for your safety. So let's thank our unconscious for doing this.

We will find that something interesting happens: when we say 'thank you', our unconscious believes we have heard it, that we are taking it seriously and it starts to work with us instead of against us. Things change, just like when we say it to other people. Things change from an argument to a conversation. From an argument where no one is listening and everyone is shouting, to a conversation where we hear each other, understand each other and work to find outcomes that work for both of us. Just learning to say 'thank you' to your unconscious can make a huge difference to how you feel. It can make a huge difference to your confidence.

So there you are: just three ways in which saying 'thank you' can make a difference to your confidence and accelerate your Confidence Journey.

## Tip 5

### Practice makes perfect: At least *deliberate* practice does

In her ground breaking book 'GRIT: The Power of Passion and Perseverance', scientist and author Angela Duckworth identified that the differentiator between successful people and those who didn't make the grade was something called GRIT. GRIT was composed of three factors: Passion, Purpose and Deliberate Practice. Having a clear purpose to motivate you and having passion for what you are doing clearly keep us going when the going gets tough. The main tip for accelerating your Confidence Journey here though is focused on one of these three factors: 'deliberate practice'.

What is deliberate practice? John Hayes, a cognitive psychology professor at Carnegie Mellon University was the first person to coin the phrase in his extensive research into top performers. He found that it wasn't just practice that led to success, but a particular form of practice. Most of us when we practice commit to doing so for a certain amount of time, regardless of the results or what we learn.

Here's a quote about deliberate practice from Aubrey Daniels, a psychologist who was one of the first people to make extensive use of behavioural analysis in business and who is often referred to as 'the father of performance management. He has many interesting articles on his webpage aubreydaniels.com:

> "Consider the activity of two basketball players practising free shots for one hour. Player A shoots 200 practice shots. Player B shoots 50. Player B retrieves his own shots, dribbles leisurely and takes several breaks to talk to friends. Player A has a colleague who retrieves the ball after each attempt. The colleague keeps a record of shots made. If this shot is missed the colleague records whether the miss was short, long, left or right and the shooter reviews the results after every ten minutes of practice. To characterise their practice as equal would hardly be accurate."

With deliberate practice we have feedback that enables us to focus our practice and maximise its value. This works for sport, art and any activity that is skill based. Guess what? Your Confidence Journey is skill based and can benefit from deliberate practice too. You can track the feedback yourself or work with friends and coaches.

- With deliberate practice, we get better at scoring our confidence.
- With deliberate practice we get better at identifying the underlying patterns on our confidence maps.
- With deliberate practice we get better at identifying our realistic and achievable desired outcome, and brainstorming options that will get us there.
- With deliberate practice we can sort through the WHAT IFs? effectively.

One of the key factors that makes it easier to practice deliberately is *knowledge*. Knowing the difference between what is good and what is not is a prerequisite for deliberate practice. This is straightforward with something like shooting hoops in basketball—if the shot isn't good, the ball doesn't go in the basket. It is also relatively easy with drawing—we can tell if what we have drawn looks like the item in front of us. It is less straightforward when looking at how we work with our teams, how we manage projects and other more complex activities.

With single loop activities, where the process is 'do it' and get instant feedback, deliberate practice can easily be done by ourselves or with one or two friends to help us out. However, many of the activities we do in our day-to-day lives are not single loop, but multi-loop. Working in a team for example is: do it, get feedback, decide which piece of feedback to take on board, do it again, see if there is a different outcome, decide if the different outcome is down to what we did or what any of the other nine people did…

Much more complex!

With multi-loop activities it is far easier to lose confidence, and much harder to gain it because that level of certainty about the 'best' way to do things is lower than with single loop activities. Knowledge helps us with this. If we build our knowledge of how projects work, how project teams work best, or how change impacts people—or just knowledge of our own self and how we react to others—all these elements of knowledge will help us in these complex situations.

How we get that knowledge makes a difference. There is a guideline in business that learning is best done following the 70-20-10 rule where 10% of the learning is from formal instruction or courses, 20% is from coaching or peer mentoring, and 70% is 'on-the-job experience-based learning'. So, to become a top project manager, join a project team led by a respected project manager and learn from seeing how they manage things. Equally, to become a top change manager, participate in a change led by someone who has experience and a good reputation for leading effective change.

By all means, read the books and do the courses—that will give you the theory underlying what you see happening in action, but learning in action is by far the most effective way to absorb useful knowledge that can then guide our own practice as then we can compare what we are doing with what we have seen these top performers do in similar situations.

Then, we can plan our own 'ladder up' strategy: we can identify a small project or change we feel we can accomplish within our Confidence Zone. We can do that project with the intent of using the experience for our deliberate practice: including having a full team debrief after the event where we can learn how we did from other people's perspectives. We can then take this feedback on board and into our next, slighter larger project. Building like this, in a short time we can use our deliberate practice to build our skills while staying within our Confidence Zone. We can continually take the next step up the ladder until we are confidently managing complex projects we thought at the start were beyond us!

With deliberate practice our Confidence Journey gets faster—and better—each time.

## Just one more thing

## About Confidence Traps and Tips

These are the top five of each, the ones I see most often either derailing someone's Confidence Journey (traps), or accelerating it significantly (tips). However, there are many more of both that you might come across. We are constantly adding to the traps and tips section on the website, so let us know if you find one and we will add it! In the meantime head on over and see if any of the ones already there are traps you need to avoid—or are tips you can use to accelerate your own Confidence Journey.

# PART 4
## HOW TO HELP SOMEONE ELSE ON THEIR CONFIDENCE JOURNEY: THE SEVEN GOLDEN RULES

Before you think about helping someone else on their Confidence Journey stop for a moment and ask yourself why? Why am I doing this? Your initial reaction to that question might be "Well it's obvious, I want to help my friend.". I am going to challenge you to pause for a minute or two and take a deeper look at this question. One of the side effects of this book, and of building your own Confidence Journey will be that you will want to share with your friends how your confidence has changed, and how you just know you can help them too.

Have you ever been around someone who recently gave up smoking, or drinking, or who recently discovered the benefits of a great new diet? How was that for you? One of the most annoying things is when someone is so full of sharing their latest discovery and how it is making such a difference for them that they don't pause to ask themselves if this is something you *want* to hear.

It's natural when something works for you to want to share and shout it from the rooftops. However, when you then start going to others and suggesting it would work for them, although you may believe it is coming from a genuine desire to help, that is not always how it is received. Research into this has shown that people who offered advice based on their own recent experiences felt empowered and engaged. That sounds great, doesn't it? How do you think the people *receiving* that advice felt? At some level they picked up on the fact that giving the advice was empowering for the giver, and in fact they felt *dis*empowered, and felt that the person offering advice was putting themselves above them, making themselves out to be a better person—and being judgemental.

Now none of these things might have been your intent, but this is how, at an unconscious level, your excitement and sharing of what worked for you and what they 'should' do can impact your friends. Does this mean you can't share what you have learned, or help your friends? No, it doesn't—however, it *does* mean that we need to follow the seven golden rules of helping others if we want to have a positive impact—and stay friends!

## Rule 1: Be a role model

The best way to help someone realise that change is possible is to be a role model for that change. If someone sees your confidence changing and growing, then they are more likely to ask you how you achieved that and seek you out for advice. Conversely, if you talk about how wonderful your Confidence Journey was and yet they see no difference, they are unlikely to pay attention to your thoughts and insights. Therefore one of the first things to think about if you want to help others with their Confidence Journeys is: how can I role model how this has worked for me? This isn't always easy. It requires a level of transparency and honesty about your own experience.

Tanya was thrilled that she had finally conquered her confidence demons. The last few presentations to senior leadership had not only gone well, she had also been right in the heart of her Confidence Zone whilst doing them. At the last event, one of her team had been there and came up to her afterwards saying, "That was a great presentation! You are so lucky to be naturally gifted at this." Tanya said to me that she had been tempted to just smile and say thank you for the compliment but something stopped her: she realised that if she did that she would be missing an opportunity to show how her own Confidence Journey had impacted her so positively. She had then spent some time with her team member sharing how scared she used to be of making these presentations, and how she had worked over many months to resolve her confidence issues and change herself. During the conversation the team member had revealed that she herself had similar fears, and asked Tanya for her support and help in dealing with them. By role modelling not only the outcome of her increased confidence, but also explaining the whole story, Tanya was able to create a connection that enabled her to help her team member on her own Confidence Journey.

In later discussions Tanya said that next time she had a confidence issue about something at work, she would be open from the start and role model how she actually worked through the process as she believed that would help her team even more. She also commented on how her working relationships with her team seemed stronger since the conversation.

The role modelling goes further than this: when helping others you will have far more impact if you ensure you role model each step on the Confidence Journey as you go through them. What does this mean? First of all it means going through the 5 steps and analysing where you can demonstrate each one:

- Do you role model scoring your confidence in situations?
- Do you use your Confidence Maps to diagnose and measure progress on your Confidence Zone?
- Do you use the IDEAS Process when faced with a problem or challenge you need to solve?

- Do you effectively role model each of the steps in the IDEAS Process?
- Do you apply Constructive Negative Visualisation to address the WHAT IFs?
- Do you practice effective planning to ensure your Confidence Journey actually happens?

I know when I have a new confidence client I often revisit the Confidence Journey to ensure my approach is as polished as possible, as only if I am an effective role model can I really add value to them.

## Rule 2: Ask permission

Have you ever shared your opinion or advice with someone only for them to ignore it or reject it? Maybe it was your partner coming home from a tough day at work and complaining about their pay and you sensibly suggested they look for another job. How did that work out? Or a work colleague comes to you over coffee and complains about a meeting they were in that just dragged on and on, and you sensibly suggest that they could speak up about this in a certain way that has worked for you in the past. How did they respond?

I know in the horse world where I see a lot of people with confidence issues, I will hear people sharing stories of how 'naughty' their horses are, and how they struggle to cope with them. However, I don't speak up and offer advice. Why? Because I have not asked their permission.

When people complain about a situation, or express concern or fear—we often assume that offering advice is the appropriate response. However, it is important to realise that in most cases, when people complain or express concern, what they are looking for is validation, not solutions. In fact offering solutions can make us appear as if we don't care about their feelings, and how the experience they are describing is affecting them. Most of the time, people want us to listen to them while they talk through the situation for themselves, and reach their own conclusions. They don't want advice.

Cameron came to me for a coaching session because he was, in his words, "Fed up with everyone trying to tell me what to do!" whenever he tried to talk about his confidence issues. With all the best intent in the world, his friends were offering stories of what had worked for them, and how they had resolved things and he had been overwhelmed and had no space to think about *his* situation and what *he* wanted to do. Coming to me was his way of finding the space to think things through for himself, with the occasional question from me to help him when he got stuck.

Quite often when we try to help our friends or colleagues, we actually end up damaging the relationship. We feel frustrated because we are trying to help and they are not seeing that, and they feel frustrated because we are not giving them the space and time to express their feelings and have their *own* experiences seen as valid and unique. A friend of mine once asked me, "How on earth am I supposed to tell if someone wants help—or a listening ear?". My answer was quite simple: ask them.

Here's how:

1. **Listen.** Let them talk freely and openly about their situation or experience without interruption, other than an occasional supporting question or empathetic comment (e.g. "How did that happen? What did you say?" Or "That must have felt horrible! That's frustrating!")

2. **Reflect.** Think about what they have said: do you feel the urge to offer a solution? STOP! Think about what is happening from *their* point of view.

3. **Connect.** By all means share a story of how something similar happened to you, that is empathy, but restrain yourself from sharing what you did about it. Sharing a similar experience builds connection. If you can't share a similar event, share your experience of the feeling.

4. **Ask**. When they have finished talking, and 'run down' a bit, pause and ask, "What do you want to do now? If you want to talk more about it I have some ideas if you like?" then listen to their response.

   Asking permission is easier if you both know the Confidence Journey structure as you can simply say, "Want to run an IDEAS Process on this?".

However, the key is:

Do they *want* to move forward?
　And...
Do they want *your help* in moving forward?

If you get permission, then you can be confident that the answer to both these questions is yes!

## Rule 3: Be truly 'other-focused'

This might seem obvious, but in practice it is not always easy to do. Our intent is to help the other person, and yet somehow, in our eagerness to help we end up focusing on our own experiences and not really listening to them. It is a characteristic of great leaders that they are consistently other-focused and see themselves as supporters, enablers, empowerers, guides, sherpas...and not as directors, instructors or gurus.

What does other-focused mean? Fundamentally being other-focused is about seeing the other person as having inherent value at least equal to your own, and behaving accordingly.

Being other-focused means taking the view that everyone is doing the best they can with the resources they currently have available, and that our role is simply increasing access to resources so the person has more power over their own life choices. Being other-focused means listening 80% of the time and talking 20% of the time. It means realising that every individual is on their own Confidence Journey that has to fit into their own particular ecology, and we have no right to impose our journey or ecology on their process.

I was coaching Belinda who was struggling to find time for her two passions, horse riding and art, since starting a new relationship. In the twelve months they had been together, she had spent less and less time on these two activities that previously had been a key part of her identity and a source of positive self esteem. It was obvious to me that the relationship was constraining her in some way and part of me was wanting to say something about this. I did ask a question: how do you think your relationship is impacting your approach to your activities? The response was a flat 'not at all', an indication to me that her ecology was not ready for her to have that conversation yet. Later in the conversation she identified that it was all to do with her mother being unwell and came up with a plan. A month later she contacted me to invite me to an exhibition of some of her artwork, and said she was riding again. She was still in the relationship that I had thought was not constructive for her. But, this was *her* Confidence Journey, and *her* ecology. Who was I to say what was more important to her? Perhaps, for her ecology, she needed to believe the relationship was solid to cope with her mother's illness? Another thought: perhaps my focus on her relationship was something from my *own* unconscious about my own stuff around relationships and nothing to do with her situation at all. As a coach I have no right to interfere with her ecology at that level. Remember, I am a coach, not a therapist, and when you are helping someone on their Confidence Journey you are a *coach*, not a therapist. I *had* raised the question, which was me being honest. However, I had to follow *her* journey, not the one I thought she should follow. Only the person in front of you knows their *own* ecology well enough to decide what will work for them.

Allowing yourself to be truly other-focused will ensure that whatever help you offer will be appropriate and genuinely supportive of their Confidence Journey.

## Rule 4: Commit to your own development

Just because you have changed a tyre once doesn't mean you are now qualified to teach people how to change tyres on any type of vehicle in any situation. It's the same with the Confidence Journey. Just because you have been through it yourself doesn't mean you know everything there is to know about the experience. It *does* mean you have an insight into how it worked for you, and maybe a head start on the principles and how to make it work. If you really want to help people build their own Confidence Journeys, then you will need to commit to your own development so you can add genuine value to the process.

How can you do this? First, study the whole of this book. Part 2 on expanding your Confidence Zone will give you lots of insights that you can use to make a significant contribution to anyone's brainstorming process on step 3 of their Confidence Journey. Part 3 will highlight the traps to be aware of, and tips that can accelerate the process so an understanding of these will also enable you to add great value to anyone's Confidence Journey.

Plus, you can do so much more: great coaches commit themselves to continuing professional development and you can do this for Confidence Journey coaching too. If you go to the website cathysirett.com you will find courses, podcasts and links to resources that will support you in this. If you enjoy helping others you can even sign up to become an accredited Complete Confidence Coach. At the very least, if a particular topic interests you, join in on the master classes on that topic where we will go into far more depth than this book's page count allows! There are lots of free resources too: on the webpage a lot of the podcasts and blogs are freely available and there is a Complete Confidence community, which is constantly building a directory of useful links, books and other resources. If the least you do is gather a deep understanding of the topics covered in this book you will already be able to make a significant contribution to anyone on their Confidence Journey, however the more you develop, the more you will have to offer both to others and to yourself.

## Rule 5: Be honest

We saw under the role-modelling rule how important it is to be honest about your own Confidence Journey. Being honest certainly means to be open and transparent about yourself and your experiences. However, it means more than that. It means to be honest when you are actually with the person you are helping. That isn't always easy, and requires courage and strength. This also comes after you have followed rules 1-4! If you have role-modelled, been invited to help and have asked permission, and are truly 'other-focused', then you are in the right place to be honest.

What does being honest mean? You may remember a story early in this book when I shared that just before I left a conversation with a friend I asked a question that had been rolling around inside my head for quite a few minutes, "How are you getting in your own way?". At the time, I wondered what the impact of the question would be, however it turned out to be the key that unlocked Vicky's door to confidence. Having the courage to be honest about the question that was in my head made a real difference to her.

That is one way to be honest: if you are working through the Confidence Journey with someone and a question keeps coming up in your head, trust that your unconscious is probably picking up on something and ask that question. Now, don't just blurt it out with no thought for the consequences as that could be upsetting—but if you think about it you can ask almost any question if you set it up or preface it appropriately. Quite often in my coaching sessions you will hear me say, "I have a question going round inside my head, and I am not sure why but I think it's important to ask, is that ok?". This way I get permission to ask it and the other person knows that it is a genuine question with their best interests at heart. One time I remember asking, "I know this is going to sound a bit off track, but I have a question in my head that seems to have nothing to do with what we are talking about here but it wants to be asked...would you be ok if I asked it?". The person nodded so I asked the question (which didn't appear to be on topic) and it struck her as relevant and very helpful. Having the courage to trust the process, and listen to your own unconscious when helping will make a real difference to your friend's progress.

Sometimes the honesty might take a different form. Remember how important it is to have a realistic and achievable desirable outcome in step 3? This is where we might have to be honest and challenge our friend's thinking and ask them: how realistic is that? How achievable is that given the reality of your situation?

Andreas was excited about his new job, which involved a move back to Madrid, his home town, as well as a change in his company and field of work. Going from financial accounting into managing company-wide projects was a big step. When he originally set his desirable outcome it was definitely a powerful goal. Within six months he wanted to be in his own house in the outskirts of the city with the children settled in their new schools and be recognised as an outstanding project manager at work.

It's great to have powerful, stretching goals. However, I had to be honest. I wondered if setting all that as a goal would put him under so much pressure that his performance would suffer. I was honest and shared my concern with him. We talked for a while and he prioritised things until his goal became "within six months I want my children settled in their new schools, and for us as a family to be settling into a new house on the outskirts of the city. At work, I want to have identified the key people and influencers to start networking with, have performed well on my first project and be ready to make my plan for progress in the company."

This was much more realistic and achievable. It also worked.

There are also times where you just have to take a deep breath and really challenge. On these occasions I will think long and hard about how to phrase things. One really enthusiastic client, Maria, was brainstorming ideas and was coming up with lots of things she could and would do. However, I was wondering how good she was at actually implementing plans. Ideas seemed to come easily to her but I had yet to see any results.

In times when I have doubts about someone's Confidence Journey I have a couple of questions I keep in my back pocket and bring out to use here. One is, "Looking at this action, when have you decided to do something similar before? How did that go? What worked well? What didn't work so well?".

This questioning was enough for Maria to realise that she was being over ambitious, and planning to do things she had never managed to complete before. However, if she remains committed to an action I have doubts about I will then drill down into the support element of the IDEAS Process and ask. "So, given that other times when you have intended to do this it hasn't worked—what has to happen *this* time for it to work?". This takes us into a discussion of what can really be effective. With Maria one particular issue was she was consistently overambitious about how much time she had to practice her talks. She would repeatedly say she would prepare and give a talk within a week and was always super stressed the day before, wishing she had more time. We identified that and broke it down into an issue around planning her talks ahead of time by proactively approaching audiences and groups rather than waiting for invitations, which always came in last minute. This was a case where me being honest with her led to significant improvements in her confidence and performance.

One thing to be aware of is the difference between being honest and being *brutally* honest. I am talking here about being honest in a supportive way, with the other person's best interests at heart. You may have noticed that I tend to frame things as questions for them to think about. I find that makes things easier to hear, and positions me as a partner in their Confidence Journey focused on helping them, which makes a difference.

## Rule 6: Make it a two-way street

How comfortable do *you* feel about being helped? Strangely, most people feel uncomfortable at the idea of being helped by someone. This is often mitigated when it is a professional relationship where we are paying someone to teach us something we don't know yet. However, when it comes to letting friends help us, most of us are reluctant to be in someone's debt, and prefer to be able to have a more balanced relationship. Just the fact of offering help can cause an imbalance in a relationship. So unless you have an existing relationship dynamic where that is appropriate (e.g. manager:employee) we need to find a way to restore that balance. How can we do this?

First of all, it is clarity about how we position ourselves and frame our help. Something as simple as, "When I was doing my first Confidence Journey, Sam helped me and it made a real difference, so I am just paying that forward," can be sufficient. You can make the balance even more powerful by actually positioning yourself as a partner in the process where you have an issue to work on as well, and their contribution will help you.

The principle of the two-way street is an important one because often, if help is not seen as balanced and two-way, unexpected consequences can occur. Have you ever helped someone—and then they have lost touch with you? Drifted away? Stopped hanging out with you so much? This is one consequence of one-way street help: at an unconscious level people feel uncomfortable with the imbalance of power and so spend less time with you and more with other more equitable relationships. By ensuring the helping is a two-way street you keep the relationship balanced and functional for you both.

I often recommend taking this even further and encourage people to find small groups to work together on Confidence Journeys. First of all this means you get lots of ideas in the brainstorming step, but also it balances out the dynamics in a healthy way as you are all in this together, helping each other and no one can be seen as setting themselves apart.

## Rule 7: Know when to get help yourself

Sometimes, even a Confidence Coach needs help. Just because I know this process inside out doesn't mean I can always do it well by myself. I often ask friends to work with me on an element—especially step 3 where the more ideas the better. So this rule is firstly about knowing when to get other people to support you on your own Confidence Journeys.

The other element though is probably even more important: know when you are out of your depth. It doesn't happen often but sometimes, when someone starts with a confidence issue it can turn into something much bigger, and that is when you need to get help.

Alison had come to me with a fear of public speaking. This was upsetting her because ever since she was a child she had dreamed of 'making a difference' in animal welfare and was now being offered the chance to take on a leading role in an animal charity. She had been on some courses, but even speaking on those had triggered such fear she was in tears every time.

We started on her Confidence Journey, but when we got to step 3 and we were identifying the desired outcome, she broke down in tears and revealed that her father had recently been diagnosed with dementia, and her mother was struggling to care for him. There were also significant issues with her siblings who, because she lived nearest, were expecting her to take on a large caring role. Now, this is not a confidence concern: this is a major life issue. We talked for a bit and we agreed that for her, seeing a counsellor would be a good next step and not to worry about the public speaking confidence until she had resolved her relationship anxieties. It is important to realise that we are confidence coaches, not therapists, and have the wisdom to advise people accordingly.

So, two forms of helping ourselves: making sure we use the support of friends and colleagues on our own confidence issues, and making sure we recognise when we are going outside the bounds of the Confidence Journey and making sure our friends get the right help at the right time.

Those are the seven golden rules for helping others with their confidence.

## Just one more thing

## What do people actually say about being helped?

To finish this section I want to share some direct comments from people I have worked with on what they wish their friends did and didn't do:

First: what *not* to do

- Tell me to just 'get on with it'. If I could do that I wouldn't have a confidence problem in the first place!
- Tell me what I should be doing. I probably know what I 'should' be doing—I just can't do it right now.
- Tell me I am wrong to be unconfident – now I feel wrong AND scared!
- Show me how confident *you* are. That just makes me feel worse.
- 'Jolly me along' in a loud voice and manner. Ignoring my feelings doesn't make them go away.
- Offer advice when I haven't asked for it. I know I may look desperate and am probably slow but I have to do it myself in my way.

- Talk about me and my confidence to other people. If you really want to help me I have to be able to trust you.
- Tell me lies. Don't say I am ok when I am not, or that I do something well when I don't. That just makes me feel even more unconfident as now I can not only not trust myself, I can't get honest feedback from you either!

Here are the most common answers on what you *can* do:

- Just be there for me. Having another person there makes a huge difference. Being ready to go for coffee with me before a big meeting, just being around, that can be a really valuable thing on some days
- Give me permission to be unconfident. When I say I am scared, let me be scared. Sure, don't let me dwell on it, but accept that right now, that is where I am…
- Give me honest feedback. Yes, there is a difference between honest and 'brutally honest' – so a bit of care how you phrase things will help, but I would rather you say, "You would benefit from some work on your intonation," than tell me I am fine when I know I am not!
- Recommend things that will inspire me. Top speakers, mentors in the company, horse riding clinics to go to. Seeing these things can inspire me to work on myself, whereas being in the same old routine doesn't.
- Help me remember what it feels like to have confidence. Sometimes it seems so long ago I forget it's possible. When you talk about the old days I remember that I *was* confident and that gives me hope that I *will* be confident again!
- Ask me if I want help. With specific things. Sometimes it is hard to say that I am worried so if you see me having difficulty, asking me if I am ok is fine and welcome!

And sometimes I will say yes, often I will say no, but just the fact you have offered will make a difference to me. Of course *how* you ask is important – a simple, "Would you like a hand with that?" will be easier to accept than anything else in most situations.

- Leave articles and books around. Lend them to me. This is far easier than talking about it in most cases – and sometimes I am stuck because I don't know what is possible. Reading an article can be a *great* help in giving me more ideas.

*There is a lot we can do to support our friends and colleagues on their Confidence Journeys, but we need to remember that it takes care and attention. Attention to the seven golden rules is a good place to start.*

# PART 5
# SUSTAINING CONFIDENCE: THREE KEYS TO STAYING CONFIDENT — AND ENJOYING YOUR LIFE

Congratulations—now you know how to build your own Confidence Journey and reach your destination, Port Confidence!

This last part of the book now focuses on making sure we *sustain* that confidence into the future. To help us do this, there are three keys to staying confident: The Confidence Wheel, and the concepts of balance and giving yourself permission.

## Key 1
### The Confidence Wheel

We have talked about how confidence is all about feeling physically, emotionally and mentally safe. We also said that one of the big five Confidence Traps is not paying attention to the bigger picture. Both of these things are important in how we can sustain our confidence.

One key way of sustaining our confidence is to use the Confidence Wheel, below.

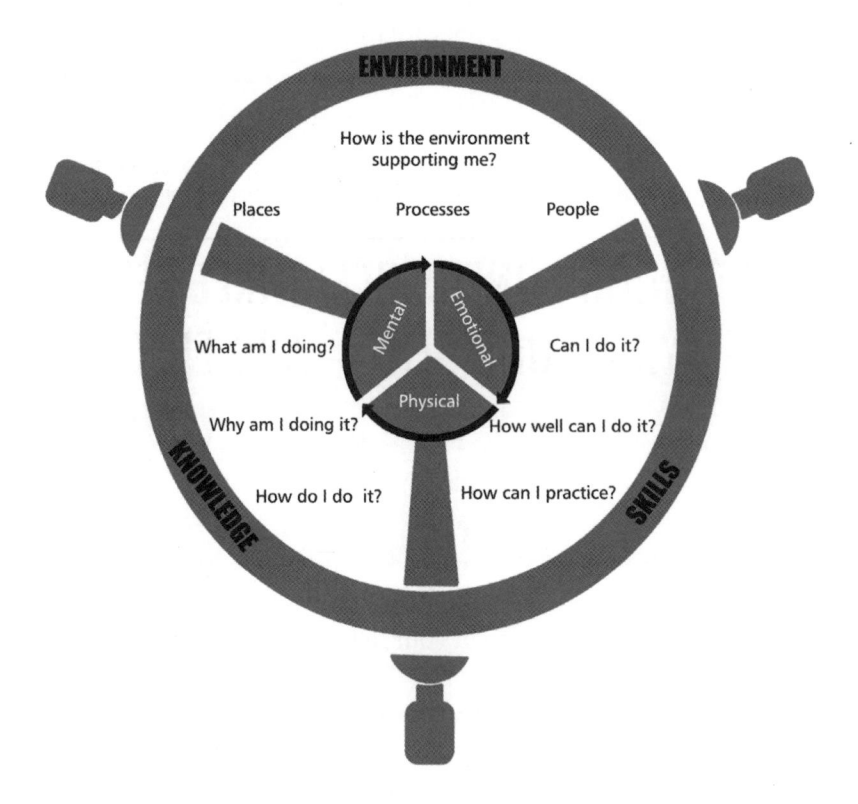

At the centre of the wheel are the words Physical, Emotional and Mental, to remind us that all three aspects of safety are important in sustaining our confidence.

Then round the outside, are the three areas where, if we ask the right questions, we can ensure we are able to stay confident in any situation.

First is **Knowledge**. We have seen how important knowledge is for our confidence earlier in this book, in so many ways. So, when we are thinking of doing something and we want to make sure we stay confident, we can ask ourselves three questions: What am I doing? Why am I doing it? And How am I doing it? Asking these three questions will show us where having a bit more knowledge will increase and sustain our confidence.

If I am asked to give a presentation, one of the first things I will ask myself is What am I doing? The obvious answer is I am doing a presentation, but if I think a bit more deeply, what does doing this presentation involve: do I have to interview people first to find out what they would like to focus on? Do I have to prepare complex slides? Do I have to have an open Q&A (question and answer) session at the end? Each of these things will mean I have to have more and different knowledge to be successful. Identifying what knowledge will help me, will also help me stay confident about the event.

Next, I will ask myself Why am I doing this? Again there is a superficial answer—'because I have been asked to do it'. However, let's go a bit deeper: am I giving the presentation because the company I am working with has a burning need for this information to be communicated? Am I doing it because no one else will step up and do it? Am I doing it because they liked my last one so much they want another one? Each answer tells me more about what I need to do to be successful. The more knowledge I have here, the better—and the more confident I will be. I also ask this question to identify how important this presentation is to me, how much it matters, so I can make sure I am putting the right amount of effort into it.

Lastly in the Knowledge section, I will ask myself How am I going to do this? If I can't answer this question, I probably need to get some support, do some research, and find more knowledge. There are so many ways to do presentations ranging from stand up at the front and use slides, to having teams at tables doing activities, to using roleplay, to having dialectics discussion groups. Have I thought about which 'how' will be most successful? And which 'how' will help me stay confident?

If I ask myself these three questions and I can't answer them adequately, that suggests that there are some straightforward

Knowledge elements I need to work on in order to be successful and sustain my confidence. Then "having these knowledge elements" can be turned into one or more desired outcomes, and I can run the IDEAS process on them to identify ways to gain that knowledge, and that confidence.

If I *can* answer them adequately, then I am all ready to move to the next section.

The second section of the Confidence Wheel is **Skill**. I can have the knowledge and know how to do something, but can I actually do it? The first question in the Skill section is therefore Can I do it? Do I know how to take the knowledge in my head and turn it into physical actions? This is a great area for anyone with physical hobbies and activities such as horse riding. We can have a lot of knowledge of what we *should* be doing, but sometimes our body doesn't cooperate with us. We know what to do but it's a completely different thing actually trying to do it! The Skill part is missing.

The next question that applies here is How *well* can I do it? It is one thing to be able to do something mechanically, so I can do it if the horse cooperates, I can do it if I have the right audience, I can do it if I get the right questions, if…if… if. It is another to be able to do it *well*, without the if's. If you hear yourself saying "I can do it if…" and there are some if's there, you are probably lower down on the scale for How well can I do it? If there aren't any if's, then you are probably much higher up that scale.

The third question on the Skill section is How can I practice? In fact, the way to increase your position on the scale for the How well can I do it? question is to practice. Deliberate practice as we discussed in Confidence Tip 5, can make a big difference to our skill level.

So, knowledge can be built by learning (from books, courses, other people—whatever works for you), skills are built by practice. Deliberate practice with proper feedback.

The third part of the circle is **Environment**: How is our Environment supporting our confidence in whatever we are trying to do?

Here there are three headings: Places, Processes and People.

The questions to ask here are first, How are the places we are in supporting us? For example, if I am practicing something I want to be in a safe place to do so. Safe physically, emotionally and mentally. When I first plan a presentation I practice by myself onto my phone voice memo or camera until I am fairly confident and then ask a trusted friend to join me and give me feedback. I make sure I stay in my Confidence Zone when doing this, and that way I sustain my confidence. Place also comes into play when thinking about how confident we will be doing something. When I ride a client's horse, I prefer to ride in an indoor, covered area first as I feel safer and more confident there. I have a friend who would hate that and prefers to ride her clients' horses for the first time out on the trail. Given what you are thinking of doing, what places would help you stay safe and confident?

Some people prefer giving presentations in large rooms with big audiences, other people prefer small groups in smaller rooms—what would make *you* stay confident?

Another aspect of this is: do *you* actually have a safe place? Do you have a place you can go to restore yourself when things get tough, challenging or anxiety provoking? This can be a physical place, or a mental place. Somewhere you can feel physically, emotionally and mentally secure. Where ever it is, we all need some form of safe place where we can go, be ourselves without judgement or criticism, where we can simply 'be' and truly relax.

The second 'P' in the Environment is Process. Do you have the right Process? Is the process one that works for you, and your confidence? It might not be the same as other people's processes, but does it work for you? This can be as simple as having a process as to what you do at which time of day. My process for writing is to have the morning as my 'free time' where I am with my horses, walk my dogs, do my errands etc and then after lunch, I settle down to think, create and write, often writing well into the evening. I still do the same number of hours as anyone else, they are just at different times in the day. When doing my business consulting, I will of course do the face to face work whenever the client requires it, but the creative, development and design aspects will be mostly done in the evenings, when my brain is working best.

How are the processes you are involved with supporting your success and confidence?

The third 'P' of the environment is People. Do you have the right people around you who are supporting you in your confidence in a constructive way, but still allowing you to make your own progress and own your own Journey? Think about the people around you, who do you share your Confidence Journey with and who do you *not* share it with? Think about your own boundaries with the people who are around you and how you can use those to create the environment that supports you in your confidence and doesn't erode it.

A friend of mine wrote a book. This was something he had always wanted to do and when he was recovering from an accident and had time on his hands, he wrote a novel about the US Civil War based on some snippets of family history he had recently discovered. He was thrilled to have written it, and excitedly shared it with family members looking forward to their reactions. When I talked to him a month later he was despondent: "They didn't like it" he said, "some said it was too violent, others said it was badly written, others said it was a waste of my time". We had a long discussion. In many cases family are not the best placed to support you on your Confidence Journey. Remember, everyone has their own issues, their own views of what is and isn't 'right' or 'good' or even 'true'. My friend realised he was better off finding some people who also wrote in this area, people who knew what this type of book was expected to be like, and sharing it with them. He did this. A month later he was delighted as they had all agreed his book had great promise and had made some constructive suggestions he was happy to take on board on his next edit.

This is the Confidence Wheel: Three levels of safety which are Physical, Emotional and Mental. The wheel is divided into three sections: Knowledge, Skills and Environment. By asking ourselves the questions in the Knowledge and Skills sections, and then asking how the Places, Processes and People in our Environment are supporting our confidence (or not!) we can make sure we sustain our confidence whatever situations or challenges we face.

# Key 2
# Balance

Just as we have talked about safety being important in three areas, physical, emotional and mental, *balance* in these same three areas is key to our ability to sustain our confidence.

Have you ever felt 'out of balance'? It's a weird feeling where things don't quite feel right, where you feel slightly out of kilter, out of alignment with yourself and the world. It's a feeling that doesn't exactly help you feel confident.

The physical aspect of balance is usually the easiest for us to understand. When we feel physically out of balance, through injury for example, we feel less confident of our ability to do things. Once we have experienced physical imbalance, we find it harder to trust our bodies again and that leads to reduced confidence. One of the roles of a physiotherapist is to rebuild our confidence in our bodies after injury. Without them, a temporary injury can turn into a long term issue.

Interestingly, with horses, physical balance has a huge impact on their emotional state and confidence. Often a horse that seems anxious and tense when ridden can be helped simply by having the rider go slower, so the horse has more time to find his balance. Once he feels safe with his balance, the horse often loses the anxiety and tension that was the initial problem.

It's the same with humans. A sensation of losing physical balance can cause us to become anxious and tense too. Working to maintain our physical balance is a key aspect of maintaining our confidence.

One of the largest physical changes experienced by a large part of the population is childbirth, and it is very common for new mothers to experience a massive loss of confidence. After all, their body has been thought huge physical changes over the past nine months, will never return to it's pre pregnancy state, and this change is challenging for many mothers. From a purely physical aspect, the body is different post pregnancy and that can impact confidence. There can be other physical causes of imbalance too, and it is always worth checking this out.

A friend of mine who was suddenly more anxious and worried than she used to be went and had some blood tests. She discovered she had an overactive adrenal gland and, once that was sorted out, returned to her usual level of confidence.

While physical balance is relatively easy for us to understand, and we can anticipate its impact on our confidence, the concepts of emotional and mental balance can be more challenging.

One piece of work that can help here is Self-affirmation theory. Developed by Claude Steele, the leading social psychologist, in the 1980's, this theory focuses on how people adapt to information or experiences that are threatening to their self concept—i.e. when their self concept is thrown out of balance. The main element of his findings was that the response to any threat was often in an area completely different to the one that was being threatened. So if someone was insulted for being a smoker, the person would not reduce or give up smoking, but instead give more money to charity when asked shortly after being insulted!

One way to visualise this is to imagine our self concept or identity as a sphere, nicely in balance most of the time (we hope!). When something happens that throws us off balance we can picture that as something poking into the sphere and pushing into it, creating a large dent. The research shows that our main focus becomes keeping the overall volume of the sphere constant, and we will do that in the *easiest* way possible for us, which often means that instead of fixing the dent, we simply bulge the sphere out in another area to compensate.

So imbalance in one area of our life causes imbalance in other areas. If you've been working on your confidence for something such as presentation skills and then one of your parents gets ill, or your private life is put into turmoil you might find you have a confidence wobble on those presentation skills. This is perfectly normal.

When we talk about emotional and mental balance, this theory comes into play as often our reaction to the emotional or mental imbalance hits us in an area where we are already weak and leaks through to give us that confidence wobble in another area unrelated to the imbalance issue.

One person I worked with was becoming more and more anxious around her horses. When we talked it became clear that she was under a lot of pressure in her life with her parents becoming older and more frail, and her partner's parents ill and needing care. Recently she had become too unconfident to ride and was just going to her horse, grooming him and then heading home again. We worked out that in all those other areas of her life she had to be the strong one, the confident one, and could not express any anxiety or stress. Everyone looked to her for support. The only area of her life where she *could* express any anxiety without affecting anyone was with her horse, when no one else was around. This was her brain's way of handling the situation. Once she realised this, she was able to put some strategies in place to have more of a balance in the rest of her life and found her confidence wobble significantly reduced.

So one of the things to always consider if you notice a change in your confidence is What's the balance in my life?

The more you can maintain balance in your life, physically, emotionally and mentally, the easier it's going to be to sustain your confidence

And if you do experience a confidence wobble have a look at other areas of your life and see if there are other ares that need to be fixed or addressed—it might not be the actual confidence issue at all!

## Key 3

## Giving yourself permission. This is the 'Just one more thing' for the whole book!

In Part 4 of the book, one of the seven golden rules for helping others with their confidence was to ask their permission. Giving *yourself* permission is the greatest key to sustaining your own confidence and enjoying your life. What do I mean by this? I mean three things:
Give yourself permission to be unconfident, give yourself permission to be confident, and give yourself permission to enjoy your life.

### Give yourself permission to be unconfident

One of the biggest challenges with unconfidence that I come across is that people don't give themselves permission to be unconfident. We spend a lot of time using the word 'should': I *should* be confident, I *should* be fine, I *should* be able to do this, everybody else can do it. All these voices constantly telling us what we should be feeling lead us to deny what we *are* feeling.

The first step on any confidence journey is to accept that we are, in fact, unconfident about something.

Let's reflect on this for a few minutes. A lot of the time we give ourselves superficial answers to the questions we ask ourselves. For example, I might ask myself "Do I give myself permission to be unconfident?" And my instant response is "Of course I do! Just the other day I felt a distinct lack of confidence about something, so I am definitely doing this!". However, there is a deeper aspect to this. It is one thing to acknowledge that we are concerned or anxious 'in the moment'. It is another to genuinely give ourselves permission to be unconfident. The easiest way to explain this is with an example of my own personal experience.

The other day I was working with a horse, and when I bent down to clean the mud out of the horse's hind feet, the horse suddenly moved as if to kick and I felt a twinge of anxiety and shot up to an 8 or 9 on the unconfidence score. To really give myself permission to experience this lack of confidence, I needed to stop and think what it was about that situation that triggered that lack of confidence. I needed to take a step back from that moment and really reflect on the specifics. Simply by doing this I am giving myself permission to be unconfident. I am taking it seriously, exploring it and not ignoring or minimising the feeling. While doing this I am, of course, realising that this is a feeling, caused by a situation, and not me being an unconfident person. Remember to make sure we phrase our unconfidence experiences in terms of behaviour and situation, not in terms of identity.

In this situation, when I analysed what it was that actually triggered the anxiety, I realised it was the surprise of his movement, I was not expecting it. When I realised this, I then asked myself if there were any other places in my life where this element of surprise triggered unconfidence. The answer was yes: I could find several examples. So by giving myself permission to have experienced the unconfidence once, I can now take it further and look at when else does that happen and from that I can start identifying a pattern. For me, that pattern was surprise and I started seeing examples of where surprise impacted me in other areas of my life. Just one example is when

I am in a meeting and someone comes up with something new and surprising, I feel unprepared and not confident about responding to it.

By giving myself permission to be unconfident, and then reflecting on similar occasions, I can actually start to identify an underlying pattern and theme. Once I have that theme, I can now address this with a Confidence Journey.

All this starts with giving myself genuine permission to be unconfident, to explore and analyse that unconfidence. If I hadn't done that, I might never had identified the underlying theme that I find surprises difficult to deal with, and they erode my confidence. Now I *know* that, I can sustain my confidence much more effectively.

When we give ourselves permission to be unconfident, allow ourselves to acknowledge this, then we can build our Confidence Journey and fix it. We can't fix it if we haven't admitted and acknowledged it!

## Give yourself permission to be confident

Sometimes we become so used to being scared and worried about something that when we actually get our confidence back we feel it's not us. Maybe other people feel its not us either. We find it difficult to meld this new confidence into our existing identity

For example, if our colleagues at work know us as someone who is not confident speaking up in meetings, it can be very challenging when we find the confidence to actually do it and speak up. It can be a bit awkward as people get used to the new us. Sometimes it's difficult for us too. It is important to see this confidence as simply a piece of our identity that was missing before, but is a genuine part of us. We are simply restoring our confidence to our default levels, repairing the damage life has done. We are restoring balance by rebuilding our confidence. This confident self is our balanced self.

So we need to give ourselves permission to go through any awkward stages and become the confident people we we truly are.

Let's take this a bit deeper too. Quite often, when I ask people I am working with to describe to me someone they see as confident, the words they use are not always positive or complimentary. Phrases such as 'arrogant', 'not listening', 'talking over people', 'bossy', 'not empathetic', 'self-centred' come up, which is a lot of negativity about what is supposed to be a positive characteristic. It's very hard to give ourselves permission to be something if we have so many negative associations with it. So here it is important to reflect on 'What is *your* image of confident people?'. Create your list of what inspires you about confident people, what excites you about them. And also create the list of what annoys you about confident people and what you don't like about some of the ones you know. Defining this means you can then decide what kind of confident person *you* want to be.

I define myself as 'I want to be confident, but not arrogant. I want to be confident speaking up but also confident enough to listen'. Agree with yourself what the identity is that *you* are happy with. What is the identity *you* give yourself permission to be when you are confident?

This is a good way of making sure we truly give ourselves permission to be confident and don't allow our negative perceptions of people who are perhaps overconfident to get in the way. Quite often we don't give ourselves permission to be confident because we have had a bad experience with someone who *is* confident and we decide we 'don't want to be like them'. So let's get those boundaries established: what is *our* definition of confident and what are we going to allow ourselves to be?

If we are to sustain our confidence going forward, it is critical to work out how we can truly give ourselves permission to *be* confident.

## Give yourself permission to enjoy your life

The subtitle of this book is 'How to build the Confidence you need to enjoy your life'. We are all allowed to enjoy our lives, so give yourself permission to be content. Give yourself permission to enjoy your rediscovered confidence and what it is bringing you in your life.

This links back to how we have voices telling us what we should enjoy and what we shouldn't enjoy. Some of us might enjoy being in our own home, with wonderful music playing, reading a good book. Someone else might have a completely different definition of an enjoyable evening and the quiet evening in might be their nightmare!

The important thing is when you give yourself permission to enjoy life, you are giving yourself permission to enjoy *your* life, not the life that other people want for you.

This can be quite challenging for some of us. It means we have to know what we want, and that is often a hard question to answer. Often, we grow up focusing on what other people want, how they want or need us to be, and don't take the time to work out and really think about ourselves and what *we* want. To help us decide what we enjoy about our lives, and what we need to be able to enjoy our lives, we need to think about what makes us content, or happy, or excited or relaxed, or joyful. Generally, we don't spend a lot of time reflecting on that. We absorb a lot from outside about what *should* make us happy, and quite often it is much later in our lives that we realise those external shoulds don't work for us, not really, and not on the inside. In fact, what makes us genuinely happy can be something very different.

This can be a challenging time for many of us as we make this transition to really focusing on what we need to enjoy *our* lives, rather than live someone else's idea of what an enjoyable life is.

Reflect on what enjoyment means for you. It can be the quiet contentment of sitting outside in your garden with a cup of tea on a nice day with a few moments of peace and quiet. It can be the enjoyment of being surrounded by loads of friends in the hubbub of a noisy party on a midweek evening and just knowing all these people are with you. It doesn't matter what it is.

You are allowed to enjoy life. You are allowed to enjoy *your* life. Give yourself permission to enjoy your life.

Thank you for buying this book. When you bought this book you gave yourself permission to work on your confidence, and that is the most powerful thing you can do.

I look forward to seeing you on the webpage cathysirett.com where there are so many additional free resources that will support you on your Confidence Journey and in sustaining your confidence going forward.

Thank you for letting me help you build the confidence you need to enjoy your life

Yours, in Confidence,

Cathy Sirett

# ABOUT THE AUTHOR

Cathy Sirett is an author, speaker and coach. She has been Confidence Coaching for 25 years in business and in life. Cathy has designed and delivered transformational change projects at organisations including KPMG, GE Finance and other multinational blue-chip clients including the leading investment banks. She has also coached and trained globally, in the UK, North America, Asia and Africa. Her focus is that most often at the heart of things is confidence: Confidence in your skills, your knowledge, your decisions and your capability. She has coached people in business, in their lives and in their passions to build their capabilities and their authentic confidence.

Cathy is the founder of Complete Confidence, a global organisation whose mission is to enable people to build the confidence they need to enjoy their lives. In this role she has worked with several organisations to enhance the confidence of their teams, including leading workshops and conferenccs. She uses her qualifications and experience with MBTI©, SDI©, NLP and Brain Friendly Learning© to enhance her work.

A classical rider herself, Cathy also works with equestrians to enable them to enjoy their passion, and have fun with their horses instead of fear.

Cathy lives in Lincolnshire, England with her two dogs, four horses and a house full of ideas, art and "enjoyable chaos".

To contact Cathy to see how she can help your organisation by speaking or leading workshops, or how she can help you build your own Confidence Journey, visit www.cathysirett.com

*Confidence Maps*

*Limiting Beliefs*

*IDEAS*

# COURSES:

*Making it Happen*

*Anchoring*

- ✓ **BUILD YOUR CONFIDENCE JOURNEY**
- ✓ **COMPLETE CONFIDENCE MASTERCLASS**

*Locus of Control*

*Fear*

Both courses are 30 days
with 6 webinars
and weekly coaching calls with Cathy!

Enroll now at cathysirett.com

Podcasts

Worksheets

Vlogs

Success Stories

**For free resources and a downloadable workbook visit www.cathysirett.com**

Examples

Interviews

Videos

Special offers